TOMORROW'S POLITICS

The Third Way and beyond

Edited by
Ian Hargreaves and Ian Christie

With contributions from:
Anthony Giddens, Charles Leadbeater, Perri 6, Tom Bentley,
Helen Wilkinson, Mark Leonard, Ian Hargreaves, Ian Christie,
Frédéric Michel and Laurent Bouvet

Other publications available from Demos:

After Social Democracy

Civic Spirit: The big idea for a new political era

EuroVisions: New dimensions of European integration

Holistic Government

The Post-modern State and the World Order

Life After Politics

DEMOS

Demos is an independent think tank committed to radical thinking on the long-term problems facing the UK and other advanced industrial societies.

It aims to develop ideas – both theoretical and practical – to help shape the politics of the twenty first century, and to improve the breadth and quality of political debate.

Demos publishes books and a regular journal and undertakes substantial empirical and policy oriented research projects. Demos is a registered charity.

In all its work Demos brings together people from a wide range of backgrounds in business, academia, government, the voluntary sector and the media to share and cross-fertilise ideas and experiences.

For further information and
subscription details please contact:
Demos
9 Bridewell Place
London EC4V 6AP
Telephone: 0171 353 4479
Facsimile: 0171 353 4481
email: mail@demos.co.uk
web site: www.demos.co.uk

TOMORROW'S POLITICS

The Third Way and beyond

Edited by
Ian Hargreaves and Ian Christie

First published in 1998
by Demos
9 Bridewell Place
London EC4V 6AP
Telephone: 0171 353 4479
Facsimile: 0171 353 4481
email: mail@demos.co.uk
© Demos 1998

ISBN 1 898309 89 2
Printed in Great Britain by Redwood Books, Trowbridge
Design by Lindsay Nash

CONTENTS

LIST OF CONTRIBUTORS

Tom Bentley is a Senior Researcher at Demos and an adviser to David Blunkett MP, Secretary of State for Education and Employment.

Laurent Bouvet teaches politics at the Institut d'Etudes Politiques in Paris.

Ian Christie is Deputy Director of Demos.

Anthony Giddens, formerly Professor of Sociology at the University of Cambridge, is Director of the London School of Economics.

Ian Hargreaves, formerly editor of the *New Statesman*, is Professor of Journalism at Cardiff University and Chair of the Demos Board of Trustees.

Charles Leadbeater is a Demos Associate and a freelance author and journalist.

Mark Leonard is a Senior Researcher at Demos.

Frédéric Michel is a researcher at the European University Institute in Florence.

Helen Wilkinson is Project Director at Demos, currently on sabbatical at the Families and Work Institute, New York.

Perri 6 is Director of Policy and Research at Demos.

PREFACE

The aim of this collection of essays is to probe further than politicians yet have on either side of the Atlantic the shape of the political agenda in the next five to ten years. Writers offer thoughts about the Third Way, as defined by Tony Blair and Bill Clinton, but this is not itself an attempt to define the Third Way. Rather, at a time of centre-left dominance in the politics of Europe and America, we offer more radical exploration of what is needed to reshape the economy, welfare, education, the European Union, eco-politics, the family, the Third Sector and the way that government works.

The collection is based to a large extent on ideas aired at a weekend seminar for Demos staff and associates on the idea of the so-called 'Third Way'. Our focus was on the challenges and possibilities for tomorrow's politics raised by the main currents of demographic, economic, environmental and attitudinal change. The participants in the seminar were: Tom Bentley, Ian Christie, Annie Creasey, Ravi Gurumurthy, Tom Hampson, Ian Hargreaves, Ben Jupp, Charles Leadbeater, Mark Leonard, Gavin Mensah-Coker, Husna Mortuza, Geoff Mulgan, Lindsay Nash, Debbie Porter, Richard Warner, and Perri 6.

TOMORROW'S POLITICS

A new political synthesis is taking shape. After a period of stasis and confusion, a modernised centre-left has won power in much of the western world. Yet its victory does not mark a simple swing of the pendulum. Instead, the centre-left has had to come to terms with a period of profound social, geopolitical and economic change that has undermined many of its assumptions. It has had to accept some of the right's agenda, while also returning to some of its own historical roots to find ideas more relevant to present and future challenges.

The definition of this new synthesis is only half complete. Some of its themes are becoming clear, but the centre-left is still a long way from having a fully formed ideological position. Instead, in countries such as Brazil, Britain, Canada, Germany, Italy and France, the search is on for a political model that can command support well into the next century.

This search is taking place within the centre ground. For now, the extremes are becalmed. In times of relative economic plenty, and with the United States alone as a superpower, the far left and the far right are largely irrelevant, though it would be a mistake to assume that primitive, populist and nationalist politics is dead or confined to faraway places. If the profound changes being wrought by globalisation of industries and market forces are mismanaged, if they are not accompanied by a sense of progress and justice, then atavistic extremism will have its chance.

So at present, the political contest is focused on how to balance prosperity with social inclusion, capitalism with community, how to modernise welfare systems, public services and labour markets, how to deepen democracy and how to connect progressive politics with the imperative of ecological sustainability.

These challenges arise against the background of profound forces of globalisation, which have sharply altered the operating environment for government. Governments can no longer easily erect barriers to the exchange of money, regulate precisely what media their citizens consume, insulate their economies from global business cycles or pursue autonomous defence strategies.

But it does not follow that governments have therefore become powerless. This is a myth, and one that is too often used an excuse for bad government. Governments do remain powerful, but they need to use their power in new ways and in those fields where they really can make a difference.

These are the fields tackled in this collection of essays. The essays represent an attempt to push the centre-left's agenda further, while also offering ideas that could be taken up by parties of the right (a further indication that the political values which are likely to animate tomorrow's voters are not easily confined by conventional party political labels).

Yet the arguments set out here are not simply pragmatic. Many claim that within what Gerhard Schröder, the German Social Democratic leader, has called 'the new middle' and others call 'the radical centre', pragmatism has replaced dogma. It is certainly true that the smarter politicians understand that socialist ends can be achieved through market means, that conservative ends may depend on interventionist government, and that green ends may depend on deals with business. This emphasis on what works is a welcome change. But on its own pragmatism is not enough. In public policy there is rarely enough information or experience to make a reliable judgement about what works: politicians need instincts and a sense of direction too.

Pragmatism is not enough in another sense as well. Governments and societies work best when they have a clear sense of values and of what they are striving for. They need the energy that comes from being able to contrast what could be, with what is. This is one reason why politics has to always be more than technocratic; why it has to be about ideals as well as about practicalities.

In this collection, we seek a route to defining the ideals of tomorrow's politics not through abstract speculation or even wide political generalisation, but through a series of essays on particular aspects of the processes of government and of policy. We have chosen this route partly because the debate sparked around the Third Way has often seemed to founder at the level of generality. Here, we start with the relatively concrete and work outwards, though the most important outcome is a set of ideas and themes, very much work-in-progress, rather than a manifesto of policies.

We make no claim to comprehensiveness, since we ignore hugely important global issues – the future of the former Soviet Union, Asia, Muslim values – and scarcely touch upon large swathes of domestic policy – prisons, transport, the media, agriculture. But because we connect specifics with values and strategy, the reader interested in subjects not covered will be able to discern an approach. What we have to say about the way that government works, about education, welfare, the third sector, the de-materialisation of the economy and the political demands of the environmental agenda has relevance across a wide range of policy fields. In short, the approach is holistic, while not attempting to describe the whole.

VALUES

We say that politics matters, that it is not just a craft, and not simply a matter of responding to public opinion or balancing interests. It has to be founded on clear values and a clear understanding of what motivates people. If it is not, people will grow more cynical and politics itself will be marginalised – always a danger in predominantly comfortable societies.

In the past, political ideals have often been deduced from views about human nature. Conservatives believed that human wickedness needed to be held in check by strong authority. Liberals believed human goodness needed to be liberated from restraints. Today we have a better understanding of the foundations of human nature. We know more about how evolution shaped our drives, our instincts, as well as our capacity to cooperate. We also know more about human potential which, for most of human history, has been held in check by the demands of agriculture and industry for unskilled, repetitive work, and by the absence of opportunities to learn, to travel and to explore that are now becoming almost commonplace for many in the industrialised world.

This essentially optimistic view of human nature lies at the root of our values, as it does at the base of the democratic tradition, the tradition of the 'demos'. It gives rise to the ideal of self-government: the belief that good societies are ones in which citizens run their own lives, living freely and with a sense of respected autonomy in communities of interdependence.

From this we derive the core founding values of tomorrow's politics, values with roots as old as the republican revolution in France 200 years ago, but adapted to today's world.

Freedom

Freedom is the foundation of self-government. Without it there is dependency and oppression. But freedom is as much a means to realising potential as an end in itself. Moreover, although we see no reason to constrain freedom in purely personal life, where our actions impinge on the well-being of others some forms of restraint are valid. Democracy and equality of respect demand that such constraints be thoroughly negotiated and applied with justice.

Equality

Democracy is founded on the idea of equal worth and equal treatment, and in democratic societies people expect equal opportunities and a set of outcomes that are widely judged to be fair. Manifestly unjust societies are prone to disabling conflicts and failure. Widespread exclusion from the core activities of citizenship, from the decent basics needed to participate in an open economy, is an indicator of serious market and political failure. Since exclusion of the poorest is causally connected to the apparently voluntary exclusion of the very prosperous from key social institutions, both are proper subjects for political action. Unbridled meritocracy results in a corrosive narrowing of what societies value and, in a time of rapid economic change, risks over-rewarding obsolete assets and achievements. There is no place in tomorrow's politics for complacency about the emergence of new forms of rigid class structure.

Cooperation

We value cooperation both at the micro level, in the family and the firm, and in society at large. Self-interest and competition are powerful forces. But they need to be channelled through frameworks of cooperation if their potential is to be exploited to best effect. A cooperative society demands that rights be matched by responsibilities – only an authoritarian or an anarchic society will set one above the other. We need especially, as individuals, as organisations and as a society, to take responsibility for the effects of our actions in relation to children, the environment and future generations.

Because these values are often in tension, we look to political institutions to calculate the trade-offs, which are not always easy to live with. So, for example, a fully-formed idea of human potential may require policies which make great demands of people, whether in education or welfare. A fully formed sense of responsibility may mean tougher obligations to manage the use of resources in an ecologically sustainable fashion. A serious commitment to cooperation may demand a new rigour in policies on business accountability and access to the law.

EIGHT STRATEGIC CHALLENGES

These are the values which guide our politics and define our ideals. By their measure we can see what is wrong with our society and outline the narrative of tomorrow's politics. That narrative is about maximising human potential and making a reality of the ideals of liberty and equality for the many to whom they now seem hollow. That means according more people more respect, but also equipping them to take advantage of more open institutions and political systems. You cannot take responsibility for yourself, your family and your community if you are disenfranchised from power inside the practical institutions of your own community: schools, housing management bodies, planning agencies and the police. For many people, the demos does not, to all intents and purposes, exist. We suggest eight defining challenges for governments at the turn of the century:

- achieving the transition to an economy based on intensive application and development of knowledge
- managing the breakdown of the old structures of the life-cycle on which much of twentieth century welfare and education were founded
- reversing the trends towards inequality and social exclusion
- protecting the environment and planning a long-term transition to an economy which is ecologically sustainable
- ensuring that science and new technologies enhance our lives rather than bringing unacceptable risks
- supporting parents and creating education systems which enable the young the thrive on the challenges of the new century
- improving mechanisms for international cooperation and democratising our systems of transnational governance
- achieving genuine equality between races, and between women and men.

These are all huge challenges. They stretch well beyond the reach of national governments. But in our view future historians will judge today's politicians by how well they understand these challenges clearly, and how much their programmes answer them.

A CHECKLIST FOR TOMORROW'S POLICY AGENDA

1. We need to understand and prepare for the new 'knowledge economy'. To every adult and child who asks how they will earn a living, there is now a new set of answers. The future belongs to those who are best able to convey, absorb and apply knowledge. This will be true not just for the obvious high-technology sectors, like computing and biotechnology, but even for quite ordinary service and manufacturing jobs, for the military, even for those whose primary work is in managing a home. The new knowledge economy will be harder to tax and to regulate and will require new forms of collaboration between the public and private sector. In chapter two, Charles Leadbeater argues for a new 'economic constitution', beyond the obvious virtues of fiscal prudence, low inflation and sensible microeconomic reform.

2. We need to acknowledge the emergence of a transformed life-cycle,
    which is undermining many of the norms and institutions which domi-
    nate our lives. Because we are living longer and requiring more educa-
    tion throughout life, it makes no sense either to require full-time public
    education between the ages of five and sixteen any more than it makes
    sense to confine public education to between the years of five and 25.
    The idea of an automatic retirement age is also obsolete – and with it
    the costly apparatus of automatic old pensions and other age-related
    benefits. The widely discussed crisis of welfare is not primarily a crisis
    of affordability, or one of morality. It is a crisis borne of changing life-
    cycles, of changing patterns of employability, and of the need to find
    new ways of achieving the goal of making people more independent for
    more of their lives. Politicians will find it hard to talk honestly about
    these issues, but the strategic need is clear: to the maximum extent pos-
    sible to use the resources of the welfare state to invest in the prevention
    of failure, rather than in the inadequate amelioration of it, as Anthony
    Giddens argues in chapter three. Radically reformed welfare policy,
    explored by Ian Hargreaves and Ian Christie in chapter four, points to
    the abolition of a fixed retirement age (and with it, the end to employ-
    ment law discrimination against older people); fiscal even-handedness
    towards saving for different purposes (education, career-breaks, parent-
    ing breaks, as well as for pensions) and to concentrate redistributive
    cash benefits on those who genuinely need them because of sickness
    and disability, or to support bringing up children.

3. Tomorrow's politics will bring a tough new agenda for institutions.
    Demos has long been concerned about the mismatch between institu-
    tions and the needs they have to fill. Too many have lost sense of their
    purpose and suffered a crisis of public trust. Rebuilding them will
    depend on many things, but these will include a much clearer mission
    and focus and clearer lines of accountability. For governments that
    means a sharper focus on achieving outcomes, and working backwards
    from those to reshape their structures, how budgets are organised, how
    innovation is encouraged, and above all how problems are solved and
    anticipated. For the electorate it means a closer engagement with how
    goals are designed, and accepting that the best thing for health may not
    be more hospitals, that the best way to solve crime may not be more
    police on the beat and that the best way to improve school standards
    may not be smaller classes. The big issue is not whether government
    should grow or shrink. Nations are viable at very different shares of pub-

lic spending in GDP. What really matters is how they spend money and how they exercise their powers. Perri 6, in chapter five, sets out the argument that government needs to define its actions by the problems it aims to solve and to focus much more political and financial effort upon the prevention of ills which otherwise are enormously costly and sometimes impossible to rectify. Holistic budgeting is among the techniques proposed, along with greater use of 'soft' techniques, such as persuasion.

4. In chapter six, Ian Hargreaves makes the argument that the third sector – not-for-profit organisations, mutuals, co-operatives and the voluntary sector – can and should play a much bigger part in our lives than the 4 per cent of GDP they currently represent. For Tony Blair and New Labour, the third sector could be as significant as privatisation was for the Thatcher government. But to unlock that potential requires a radical agenda to create a legal and regulatory framework for third sector organisations that will enable them to expand their role. He proposes: a network of 'social capital banks' around the country, to provide risk capital for the sector; the rewriting of charity law; and new incentives for collaboration between business, the third sector and the state.

5. Education is an acknowledged priority of the current British government and most other governments. Tom Bentley, in chapter seven, goes back to the ideas of Ivan Illich to propose 'de-schooling' as part of a set of ideas to create a 'learning society' appropriate to the emerging knowledge economy. Today's mechanistic approach to education, he argues, ignores advances in the understanding of the nature of intelligence and fails to teach pupils the most crucial skill: how to relearn and how to apply knowledge. More and more, learning will have to take place in the contexts where knowledge is actually used and valued, rather than being hidden away in institutions. His specific policy proposals include: the right of parents to claim back the cost of a child's education to create their own school; assessment of educational performance by external bodies, such as employers; and the use of school buildings for a wide range of community purposes.

6. Tomorrow's politics must have the courage to put a radical environmental agenda into practice. Too much scaremongering, too little attention to real interests, a romantic attachment to the past and too little concern with practical politics have all seriously flawed the green move-

ment's ability to fulfil its promise, despite its great achievements in the past 30 years. But mainstream politics has also failed to match green rhetoric with deeds. What is now needed is a much sharper programme of ecological modernisation: aiming to achieve truly sustainable development; using science and technology to transform materials and energy efficiency in the economy; reshaping tax systems to cut energy use and promote the integration of environmental factors into business planning. But eco-modernisation is not simply about environmental protection and improvement. Ian Christie's core message, in chapter eight, is that it can help achieve other goals central to tomorrow's politics. Ecological tax reform and new approaches to planning for sustainable development could help increase employment, improve quality of life and help reconnect citizens to the democratic process in his proposed new 'ecopolis'.

7.   Helen Wilkinson's argument about the family, in chapter nine, also picks up the theme of preventive politics. She argues that family policy has for too long been dominated by unconstructive debates between traditionalists and liberals. A fresh approach to the family will recognise that 'family values' do indeed need to be supported, but not in a rigid and prescriptive top-down fashion. She argues that, in future, the most powerful reasons for supporting stable and cohesive families will be their contribution to long-term public health and social capital: not only is divorce bad for many children, but solid, enduring relationships are good for adults and the wider community, including employers. Our capacity to make and maintain such relationships and raise children successfully should therefore be encouraged by a number of policy initiatives, including new forms of community information and support services for parenting; policies for family-friendly employment, such as paid parental leave; innovations in marriage preparation; and a focus on fathers as much as on mothers in family policy.

8.   Mark Leonard's essay (chapter ten) examines the capacity of the European Union to contribute to meeting the challenges to transnational cooperation posed by the key problems raised in these essays. He argues that for all its successes, the project of European integration now faces deep-seated problems of legitimacy, efficiency and strategic direction. These, he claims, are rooted in the lack of arenas and mechanisms for democratic political conflicts about the future of Europe. He proposes a set of institutional innovations designed to inject more constructive

conflict and democratic participation into the system without creating cumbersome federal institutions. He argues that a new course for Europe can be based on the unique strengths of the Union as a collaborative network of states and organisations rather than an embryonic state or federation.

9. In chapter eleven, Frédéric Michel and Laurent Bouvet offer a view from the continent of the Third Way debate. They conclude that there is greater convergence than sometimes seems to be the case between the Blairite Third Way and the attempts at renewal of social democracy in Germany and Italy, and even in France. But because most continental governments operate in coalitions, they tend to proceed through channels of negotiation with the social partners which are out of favour in Britain. They suggest that with the centre-left in almost unchecked political control of Europe, however, an evolving process of modernisation for social democracy is more likely than any radical departure in the direction of New Democrat liberalism. If Britain wishes to be closely engaged in the European Union, it will have to learn from continental social democrats as well as preaching to them.

THE POSSIBILITY OF PROGRESS

What underpins many of these essays is a simple idea: that tomorrow's politics needs to recapture a sense of *progress*. Earlier this century, most people felt they were part of a great narrative of enlightenment and civilisational progress. Each generation assumed that it would be better off than the last one, better educated, healthier and freer. Now this view has become unfashionable, and not without reason. A century when unprecedented prosperity has been combined with massively destructive warfare, environmental destruction and chronic inequality, has shattered many people's faith in the future. Any idea of progress today has to be conditional.

Yet for all the profound problems of the twentieth century, there has been continuing, and by the standards of past generations, extraordinary progress for many people. The simplest measures are those of life expectancy, health, learning and income. Other measures include the spread of democracy, or the richness of modern moral argument (how many past generations debated so seriously the rights of animals and the biosphere, the needs of women, the need to respect other religions?). We also have available more knowledge and more opportunities for learning than at any point in the past: resources which could allow us to learn and communicate how to do things better to more people than ever before.

It is important to keep this bigger picture in view because losing a sense of progress can have a serious and direct cost. Societies with a strong sense of the future bring out the best in people. In traditional societies, this sense was achieved through religion and ritual that situated the individual in an unbroken chain linking ancestors and descendants. Today the idea of progress is our nearest equivalent for encouraging more caring, more responsible, more moral and less selfish behaviour.

Yet many of today's pressures make it appear as if we live in an eternal present. Our two dominant decision-making structures – the consumer market and representative democracy – are particularly oriented to the present; and our dominant source of information, the mass media with which the typical adult spends 30 hours each week, have only a very limited sense of history and depth.

A politics for tomorrow involves a mission that goes beyond just satisfying demands and balancing interests. It has to be serious about investing in children, in education, in preventing great problems whose outlines we can discern. It has to be serious about encouraging everyone to take responsibility for their own future, through accumulating skills and saving for old age. It has to be serious about the environment, and the quality of the legacy we leave to the next generation. And it has to be serious about fiscal responsibility, and not dumping debts on to our children.

These points may seem unexceptional. But they clearly define the enemies of tomorrow's politics. Reaction, fundamentalism, monopolistic interests, inflexibility, short-termism (whether in business or government) and an obsession with purely economic inputs and outputs which, in the end, devalues the sacred idea that every individual is entitled to be a full member of the polity and of society.

The ideals of liberty, equality and cooperation are not new, but they remain only partially achieved. They still have the power to inspire and to set a benchmark against which we measure our progress. More than ever, they point the way to using collective power to achieve better, more fulfilled lives for all. This is what politics is for.

WELCOME TO THE
KNOWLEDGE ECONOMY

Charles Leadbeater

Imagine Bruce Willis failed in the film *Armageddon* and the earth were hit by a meteorite which returned the world to the physical state it was in 4,000 years ago. Every physical manifestation of the modern world would be destroyed, apart from the US Library of Congress, with a full stock of the world's books and journals. It would take perhaps three generations for living standards to return to the levels they enjoyed for most of the twentieth century. Now imagine the same meteorite wiped out everything, including the Library of Congress. After this shock, the earth's economic recovery would take far longer, perhaps several centuries. The difference is one measure of how valuable knowledge has become. Physical infrastructures and raw materials matter, but they become really valuable when they are combined with knowledge of how best to use them.

Take another example. The personal computer I am using to write this essay has about the same amount of plastic, gold, silicon, copper and other metals as the computer I used five years ago. Both machines weigh and look much the same. But today's machine is twenty times more powerful than the older machine. The difference is entirely to do with the way the physical components have been rearranged. That difference comes from human intelligence, rearranging the available physical materials to make them more productive. That is the story of modern economic growth. Improvements in productivity and wealth largely come from human ingenuity: our finding cleverer ways to combine the basic physical components available to us on or just below the earth's crust.

Take two more examples: the humble drinks can and a blade of wheat. Twenty or 30 years ago, drink cans were so heavy it took an act of strength to crush them. These days drink cans are made of ultra-thin, ultra-light material. The can's shape is maintained in large part by the liquid inside it. Today's drink can is 80 per cent lighter than twenty years ago because science has allowed it to be made of lighter materials. The modern can is 80 per cent know-how, 20 per cent materials. Knowledge has replaced metal. Similarly, the average blade of wheat is 80 per cent more productive than wheat in the 1930s because scientists and breeders have learned how to grow more productive, robust strains. The modern grain of wheat is 80 per cent know-how.

These examples show how knowledge has become a central, perhaps *the* central, ingredient in economic growth in developed economies. The cellular telephone, for example, combines at least five different kinds of technology, about which most of us understand very little. In future, the central component of economic growth and well-being in the developed economies is unlikely to be population growth, raw materials, land or physical plant and equipment, the assets which fascinated economists in days gone by. The engine of growth will be the process through which an economy creates, applies and extracts value from knowledge. The task of modern economic policy is to foster the twenty-first century knowledge economy.

The centre-left in Britain and elsewhere needs to grasp this historic opportunity. It is not that everyone will suddenly start working in white lab coats researching new genetic cures for cancer. These high-tech industries, based on the rapid transmission of science into commerce, will certainly be at the leading edge of the knowledge economy, generating wealth and jobs in other service industries. But over time, even quite hum-drum jobs in services and manufacturing will themselves become more knowledge intensive. The factory of the future will be more like a 'knowledge works', combining research, marketing, engineering and innovation.

It is a transition that will involve sweeping changes to many institutions of economic life inherited from the industrial era: the joint-stock company, traditional accounting, competition policy, taxation, the role of universities. Yet the centre-left seems caught in a trap over economics, a trap almost entirely unwittingly laid by modernisers, myself included. If the centre-left is to command the political agenda for more than a few years, it has to spring this economic trap. It has to develop not just economic policies, but an economy story to show why it is uniquely well-placed to tap the knowledge economy's potential for growth, innovation and productivity.

What the centre-left needs is not a hard edged economic theory, of the sort that Margaret Thatcher drew from monetarism. Rather, it needs a coherent account of the capacity and limits of macroeconomic management and an understanding of how the economy can be refashioned to make firms and people better able to create knowledge-rich products and services. For that, we need to describe what might be called an 'economic constitution' – setting out a balance of powers between markets and the state, the public and private sectors, to promote both flexibility and security within an economy open to the global market.

The phrase 'economic constitution' makes it sound high flown. But just as a political constitution has to pay out in terms of individual rights and entitlements, for example to vote in elections, so an 'economic constitution' has to make sense to people in terms of their jobs and livelihoods. At its most basic, the government has to be able to tell a story about how the economy will develop that will help people to make sense of how they and their children will make their living, what sort of companies they will be working for, making what sorts of products and using what sorts of skills. People want a sense of where they are going and how the government's economic policies will help them to improve themselves. The task is to provide the economic constitution for the knowledge economy.

The Blair government, in common with centre-left governments around the world, has the makings of such an aspirational, optimistic, narrative of economic improvement but it has not yet been fully articulated. The government thus far has relied on telling an economic story of prudence, stability and competent management. This narrative is also essential: a recession would undermine the government's claim to competence and its policies on social exclusion, welfare-to-work and equality of opportunity. But just as high quality is now regarded as essential for all world-class manufacturers, so prudence and stability cannot be a sufficiently distinguishing feature of centre-left government. All governments must aim for prudence and stability. The question is how to combine a track record for macroeconomic competence with a distinctive approach to economic modernisation.

THE MAKINGS OF THE TRAP

It was a watchword of modernisation on the centre-left in the 1980s that it had to recognise basic economic realities before it could ever again command power. First, the left had to wake up to the power of international markets, which circumscribe the role of traditional macroeconomic policy in promoting full employment. It became indisputable in the 1980s that the market is the most effective way of coordinating much of the economy and, in most areas of economic life, is far superior to centralised planning and state ownership. Second, nationalisation had had its day. Renationalising privatised companies was expensive and of doubtful value. A mixture of privatisation and regulation seemed to serve the public interest well. Modernisers stressed that how a service was owned was less important than whether it delivered the desired outcomes. Third, the modernisers renounced the centre-left's love affair with tax-and-spend policies. The left had to acknowledge not only a widespread unwillingness to pay more tax, but also a widespread scepticism about whether the state could spend it productively. Even when the public sector had abundant resources – for example, the police in the 1980s – the result was often poor efficiency and failure to adapt.

This modernising position helped to show that the centre-left recognised how the British economy was affected by the global economy and that the old class politics, based on unions and manufacturing industries, was no longer tenable. The centre-left had to appeal beyond its traditional class support because economic change was wiping out its old strongholds. This modernising credo helped to defeat the old left and establish Labour's credentials as competent, realistic economic managers. The endorsement of economic orthodoxy left Labour well placed to profit from Tory blunders.

This was the economic position that carried Labour into government, where it has led to important changes, among them independence for the Bank of England, new rules for fiscal policy and a three-year comprehensive spending review to put public spending on a more predictable footing. Yet this approach has also left the government seemingly defending the economic orthodoxy of free trade, flexible labour markets and enterprise, combined with fiscal prudence and stability. There are divergences from Conservative policy – such as the minimum wage – but as yet, the government's economic policies do not pull together into a distinctive narrative of how the economy should develop.

In particular, the modernising credo has brought in its wake three problems. First, while ministers seem at ease talking the language of prudence and public spending control, they are far less at ease talking about entrepreneurship and risk taking. Labour still seems most at ease with a world of large, heavy-weight organisations – an impression confirmed by the stream of big business executives brought into government task-forces. The centre-left needs to be more at ease with the young, disestablishment, knowledge entrepreneurs who are creating the companies of the future.

Second, one of the government's central economic claims is that it will end the 'boom and bust' cycle which brought us two recessions in a decade. This claim, always a triumph of hope over expectation, will become impossible to sustain if the economy slides downhill in the coming year.

Third, apart from the general and quite correct support for education, there is no distinctive account of how the centre-left will develop the economy's wealth-creating capacity. The government has criticised manufacturers for poor productivity but proposes no remedies. The government has talked at times of Britain as a 'creative economy' but that phrase identifies it too much with the 'Cool Britannia' industries of fashion, music and design, important though those are.

This lack of a distinctive Big Picture story of how the British economy will develop threatens to leave a hole at the heart of the centre-left's politics. It is as if the structure of the economy is off limits, best left to the market and private companies, leaving the government to promote education to help people compete better in the modern economy and to modernise the welfare safety-net to help people get back into work if they lose their job. As a result, the centre-left's politics seem unbalanced: focused on social issues such as education, health and welfare rather than the structure of the economy. This allows critics to allege that New Labour will simply pick up the pieces left behind by the global market; that it is warmed up Thatcherism; that it does not add up because its adherence to market orthodoxy will make it impossible to create a more cohesive society. Proving these critics wrong will require more than repeating the mantra of prudence and stability. It will require the government, and the centre-left more generally, to develop its own distinctive account of how the economy should be structured, the economic constitution.

WELCOME TO THE KNOWLEDGE ECONOMY

The asset base of the economy is shifting. The traditional assets of economies since the days of Adam Smith – land, labour, raw materials, machinery – are becoming less critical to competitive advantage. Intangible assets – know-how, creativity, brands – are becoming increasingly critical.

One sign of this is the gap that has opened up between the value accountants give to a company's physical assets and the value put on a company by the stock market. To take an extreme case, only about 6 per cent of Microsoft's market value is accounted for by fixed assets recorded in its balance sheet, such as buildings, furniture, equipment and computers. About 94 per cent of the value of the most dynamic company on the world is stuff that cannot be measured, weighed or pinned down: research and development in progress, brands such as Windows, and people, Bill Gates and his chums. Take another example: in 1995 when IBM bought Lotus, maker of the Lotus Notes programmes, it paid $3.2 billion. Of that, $1.84 billion went on research and development in progress: that is ideas and people. A recent Brookings Institution study of more than 2,000 US manufacturing firms found that physical tangible assets accounted for just one-third of their stock market value in 1994. A decade earlier, book assets accounted for close to two-thirds of the value. This is not just a US phenomenon. Similar figures emerge from studies of other economies.

Intangible assets are becoming more important in economic development for several reasons. First, we are producing unprecedented amounts of scientific knowledge and translating this more quickly, into more areas of commerce and production. Perhaps the best example of this is biotechnology. Biotech research has been made hugely more productive by bio-infomatics, computer-based methods of searching for new gene strings and compounds. The results of this research are being translated into products within months of their discovery. Just after the Second World War, the transmission time between scientific discovery and product development was at least a decade. We are in the gestation phase of entirely new industries, many of them based on biology, that will create families of new global products in the next century: bio-materials, neuroscientific treatments and nanotechnology.

Second, the semi-conductor is becoming ubiquitous and vastly more powerful. This allows us to collect information about a much wider range of activities. Computerisation has made production more efficient, but it has also allowed companies to enter into information-rich exchanges with customers. When the world is awash with information, merely being able to collect information will no longer be a competitive advantage. The task will be to anticipate the future. The best companies require small amounts of the right kind of information to make good judgements. Bill Gates is not a success because he can process more information than most people. Gates, at the moment at least, seems to be a master of pre-cognition. He is able to discern the emerging shape of competition from the fog before everyone else.

Third, competition is driving companies towards knowledge and other intangible assets as the distinctive base for sustainable competitive advantage. It is difficult to maintain a competitive advantage in a world of free-flowing information and capital, which allows competitors to copy production technologies or products. Many production components in industries such as electronics can be bought on open markets. What manufacturers must add is the ability to put these components together in cleverer ways. And new technology is breaking down barriers to entry which used to protect industries. Banks, for example, have found that traditional physical assets – a high street branch network – have become, in part, a liability in a world of electronic and telephone banking. Companies operating in increasingly competitive markets need to base their competitive position on know-how, creativity and branding. These assets are difficult for competitors to imitate. Of course it is not knowledge on its own that counts, but how it is combined with the financial and physical resources to realise its value. Intel is successful not just because it produces a stream of innovative semi-conductors, but because it can afford to spend $3.5 billion on its next chip making plant.

Intangible assets are not marginal or an unproductive service tail to a small, highly productive manufacturing sector. In the 1990s, services contributed five times more than manufacturing to UK growth. Demand for unskilled labour has collapsed. The wage differential for those with skills has risen markedly since 1980 despite an increase in the supply of graduates. In 1980, a man with a first degree or above was paid 148 per cent of the median earnings for all males. In 1993, the figure was 156 per cent. Over the same period, the wages of those without a qualification or with a GCSE below grade one fell respectively from 91 per cent and 98 per cent of median earnings, to 81 per cent and 85 per cent. Professor Baruch Lev of New York University's Stern School of Business estimates that the US manufacturing industry's investment in intangible assets, such as research and development, training and brand development, is worth about $210 billion a year: roughly the same as the amount that US manufacturers invest in physical plant and equipment.

A NEW POLITICS FOR THE NEW ECONOMY

More of the products we consume and the assets we use are intangible and knowledge intensive. It no longer makes much sense to talk of Britain as an industrial or service economy. Its aim should be to become a distinctive knowledge economy, trading on its know-how whether that is delivered through manufactured products or services. The role of government economic policy should be to ease Britain's passage into this knowledge economy. That does not mean Britain will cease to be a manufacturer. It does mean that modern manufacturing will become increasingly knowledge intensive. The manufactured products we buy – diskettes being a prime example – are physical vehicles for intangible value. Promoting Britain as a knowledge economy does not mean that everyone will be working in high-tech biotechnology companies. Most people will be employed, probably by quite small companies in the service sector. But the leading edge of the economy – biotech, software, communications, design – will be knowledge intensive, and more of what follows in its wake – banking, pharmaceuticals, engineering, products related to eco-modernisation – will become increasingly knowledge intensive.

What does this shift mean for economic policy? The central narrative is clear. In future, economies will compete on their ability to acquire, generate, apply and exploit knowledge. Modern economies will be made up of overlapping knowledge supply chains, which will help to take ideas from inception through to commercialisation. Successful economies will need a rich and deep knowledge base of well-educated workers and world-class research. But education is just an enabler. The critical question for economic policy is how a knowledge base is exploited and developed, how ideas are turned into products and businesses. This process – generating, applying and exploiting knowledge – will become the driving force for modern economies.

Many of the traditional goals of centre-left economic policy will be highly relevant to this new economy: to help prevent markets from undermining themselves or spinning out of control; to expand the winners' circle; to humanise capitalism. But the rise of the knowledge-based economy means that these goals will need to be pursued in a different way.

The good news is that this emergent economy is, in important ways, more in tune with the values of the centre-left than those of the new right. Knowledge creation thrives on sharing and collaboration as well as competition and individual creativity. At its very roots, a knowledge economy needs sustained public investment in the intellectual infrastructure of education, research and communication. The knowledge economy, for reasons which are written into the nature of its assets and products, will have a large, public, collaborative dimension. It will not be the sole preserve of traditional private sector companies.

The best guide to the scale of reform that the shift to the new economy will entail is the institutional innovation which helped to unlock the potential of the industrial revolution in the nineteenth century.

The nineteenth century was a revolutionary period in industry and commerce not just because it gave us the telegraph, the train, the car, the telephone, the aeroplane, the cinema and machines of all shapes and sizes. The potential of these technologies was unleashed by a new generation of institutions designed to make the most of these new industrial assets. Technological innovation was matched by institutional and organisational innovation. Although technology has moved on in leaps and bounds in the late twentieth century, we are living largely with our institutional inheritance from the nineteenth century. In the UK, the joint-stock company reached legal maturity only with the 1862 Companies Act, and only in the 1880s did it become the dominant form of capitalist organisation. Consumer cooperatives and burial associations became the basis for the modern building societies, given legal form in the friendly society and building societies law of 1874. Trade unions gave voice to labour in the late nineteenth century and institutions of higher education, incorporating scientific research, were created as the century progressed. What we should admire about the Victorians is not just their technological innovation, but their capacity for matching this with institutional and political innovation.

By contrast this century has been lopsided. Although technological and scientific innovation has accelerated, institutional and organisational innovation has been pitiful. Our institutional innovation has been incremental, while our technological innovation has been radical. The centre-left is in danger of embracing a cautious economic orthodoxy at just the time when it should be embarking on a radical modernisation of many of the core institutions of the economy to help bring the knowledge-based economy to life.

POLICIES FOR THE KNOWLEDGE ECONOMY

The rise of the knowledge economy will touch all aspects of our lives and should refashion much of government policy. For example, the growth of electronic commerce and electronic money will change how taxes can be levied and collected. Competition policy may need to be rewritten to take account both of the threat of new global monopolies, such as Microsoft, and also the increasingly important role of innovation. Traditional competition policy was designed for a world of steel and rail barons, not biotechnology entrepreneurs. Legislation and regulation often lags several years behind the fastest moving industries. Insider trading rules may need to be amended because knowledge intensive industries, such as biotechnology, are so hard for outsiders to fathom and relatively easy for insiders to profit from.

Entrepreneurship, the ability to make the most of your individual skills and assets, will become a core skill in the new economy, in both large and small companies. Entrepreneurship therefore needs to be one of the most vital skills imparted by our education system. The pace of technological change is constantly creating new opportunities for business. To take one example, the British computer games industry is one of the most successful in the world, built entirely by software entrepreneurs below the age of 40 and many below the age of 30.

What follows highlights five broad areas where the government needs to start writing the economic constitution for the knowledge economy.

- *Innovation.* Economies will compete on their ability to generate and apply know-how. This process of innovation will not be conducted by companies alone or even by groups of companies but by knowledge-creating networks in the economy. The best example of how these networks operate is in Silicon Valley, California, where the universities of Berkeley and Stanford are constantly producing new ideas and entrepreneurs, which venture capitalists help to translate into businesses. Large companies, such as Microsoft and Sun Microsystems, frequently buy into these small start-ups and provide the financial and marketing clout to take their ideas to market. The emergence of these knowledge-creating networks has four implications for economic policy. First, innovation in modern economies takes place in networks that link universities, entrepreneurs, finance and access to consumer markets. The unit of competitiveness in the modern economy should be the network, not the company or the sector. Second, these networks are partly public and partly private. Universities will play a critical role providing the knowledge base for many modern industries: they could become hubs of the knowledge economy. Third, these networks do not thrive on an economic culture of pure individualism and competition. They thrive on a mixture of cooperation and competition. Silicon Valley, for example, is intensely competitive. That is what drives people on. But it is a success because its networks also organise the distribution of know-how and ideas among a community of professionals. These networks organise the sharing and distribution of knowledge as well as its exploitation. Finally, networks rely on a matching set of political institutions. They cannot thrive through private sector endeavour alone. In the high-tech cluster around Cambridge, for example, the biggest constraints on growth are all in the realm of public policy: housing, transport, the environment. These networks are usually regionally based, so that ideas and people can move fluidly. Creating the environment for such knowledge-creating networks to flourish then is a vital task for more devolved regional economic management.

- *Inward investment.* Inward investment from Japan was one of the few success stories of industrial policy in the 1980s. Britain did not just import technology and equipment: it also imported Japanese know-how and techniques for just-in-time production. The importation of this know-how will have a more lasting effect on the British economy than the factories and machinery, which will be written off in a few years. What will be the equivalent of this manufacturing-based inward investment policy for the 1990s? In the knowledge economy, Britain will have to import people and ideas. Britain needs to become the most attractive place in Europe for talented people to work and gather. Silicon Valley has a *de facto* industrial policy: it cream skims the best talent from the most prestigious universities in the world. In the US, the most contentious issue in industrial policy are the restrictions on the visas allowed for foreign workers, which US companies are constantly pressing to be relaxed to allow them to import more brain-power, more raw material for the knowledge economy. Britain needs to learn from this. One measure of how far behind we are is the experience of the research laboratories of a British company such as

Glaxo-Wellcome. In Glaxo-Wellcome's US research labs there are scores of very bright, ambitious Malaysian researchers. In the UK there are at most a handful. The most successful modern inward investment policy has been pursued by the English Football Premiership. Using money raised from the sale of television rights (itself an intangible asset) the Premiership clubs have imported some of the best footballers in the world. The Premiership has become a place where some of the best talent in the world congregates and competes. We need to follow the Premiership strategy in other areas of the economy. In the knowledge economy, industrial policy and immigration policy are inseparable. The Home Office, it turns out, not the Treasury or the Department of Trade and Industry, controls our access to some of the richest assets in the knowledge economy: foreign talent.

- *Ownership.* The issue of ownership was thought to have been put to rest by the privatisation programme and the de-mutualisation of most building societies. It seems that the publicly quoted private company has emerged as the natural dominant organisation. Yet just as it was assumed that the issue of ownership had been settled, the knowledge economy will open it up again. Take three issues where ownership will once again become contentious. First, the know-how that companies will use to compete comes from people. Human capital will be the source of the most valuable assets in the modern economy. The most successful modern companies will be hybrids, owned by both human and financial capital. The implication of this is a radical extension of the rights of employee ownership and equity pay. About 23 per cent of Microsoft's issued equity is under option to its employees. In the UK the limit is 3 per cent. Second, the knowledge base for the industries of the future is largely publicly funded and owned. Much of it lies in university research labs. Again, the likelihood is that we need to develop new hybrid institutions, both public and private, to make sure this knowledge is both shared and exploited. Private companies are good at exploiting knowledge but poor at sharing its development. Public institutions are quite good at sharing knowledge but poor at exploiting it. Public–private hybrids could combine the strengths of the two organisations and minimise their weaknesses. This will open up the whole issue of how universities and their intellectual property should be owned. Third, the rise of industries built on biology will pose troubling ethical questions about who should own the knowledge on which they are based. Take genetics as an example. A gene is nothing more than a string of information, developed through millions of years of joint-evolution. Should a company be able to patent a gene or its applications? Who should own our genes? Do they belong to us or our ancestors? The US biotechnology industry has grown rapidly in the past decade in part because the US Patent Office has allowed companies to patent genes and other naturally occurring biological phenomena. The US Patent Office is one of the most important ingredients in a new industrial policy for the biotech sector. The issue of intellectual property rights will move from the margins to the mainstream of economic policy-making.

- *Value*. One reason the new right emerged triumphant in the 1980s was that it seemed to have the only convincing account of how economic value was generated and measured: value was the price arrived at through unadulterated market exchange between free consenting adults. The value of something was the price it would fetch in an open market. In contrast, the left has always struggled with a theory of economic value. The labour theory of value, whatever its intuitive insights into the workings of capitalism, ended up going round in ever decreasing circles when applied in detail. Yet in many ways the pendulum is swinging away from the new right, because it is clear that the market is not a good way to account for the value of many of the products and assets of the new economy. First, markets are poor at transacting knowledge. You cannot test drive a divorce lawyer. Because know-how is fuzzy, tacit, personal and dependent on context, its value cannot be easily specified in a contract. As a result, markets are often a poor way to organise the distribution of know-how; networks and other collaborative arrangements become more important. But that in turn means that traditional, market clearing models of pricing and value are not relevant. It is also increasingly clear that traditional financial accounting and the system of national accounts is next to useless at capturing the value of this new economy. The traditional system of accounting was designed for a world of trade in commodities. But the service sector, both public and private, dominates the British economy. Its most important assets are intangible: people, skills, a brand image. Yet the assets that are recorded on the balance sheets of these service companies are tangible and physical assets such as buildings, cars, computers, furniture. Armies of accountants are paid to draw up these balance sheets and yet they are next to useless as a guide to business performance. An entire industry – accountancy – is based on a fiction: that the numbers auditors produce measure the sources of wealth and value within the companies they audit. The new knowledge economy will require us to develop new measures of value and economic performance.

- *National security.* One way to measure what is most valuable to us is to work out what we would defend in a war. How do you defend an economy in which the most important assets are no longer mainly factories, railways and physical infrastructure? The geography of the British aerospace industry is almost entirely shaped by the need to relocate factories beyond the range of Second World War German bombers. These days most of our vital infrastructures – electricity, communications, water, transport – are controlled by networks of computers, which could be hacked into. The vital economic assets we need to protect in the intangible economy are intangible: information, computer networks, communications systems. These systems can be attacked by computer from anywhere in the world. A striking illustration comes from the military world where, since the Gulf War,

'we have seen a transformation from the mechanised warfare of the information age, to the information warfare of the information age. Information warfare is a war of knowledge and intellect. The aim of information warfare is not to wipe out the enemy but to control your opponent, using electronic warfare, network sabotage and psychological warfare. The aim is to vanquish the enemy not by fighting, but through a "soft-strike".'

The quote comes from Jiefangjun Bao, of the Chinese Army Newspaper, reporting on the strategy outlined for the Military Strategies Research Centre in Peking when it was inaugurated in 1996.

CONCLUSION

The centre-left has got itself out of the big hole it dug in the 1970s when it seemed out of date and out of touch, saddled with an economic policy which lacked credibility. The centre-left in the UK and elsewhere has painfully regained public credibility and trust by acclimatising to the market and international competition, and accepting the case for fiscal prudence and low inflation. As far as macroeconomic management goes, the centre-left has learned its lesson. And it has combined this reputation for competence with sensible supply-side policies, on welfare-to-work and education.

But this reputation for competence is fragile and recently won. It could well be undermined by a downturn. The danger is that the downturn will arrive before the centre-left has developed a compelling and distinctive narrative to identify itself with economic improvement and wealth creation. It will need such a narrative if it is to dominate the political scene for more than a handful of years.

The task for the government is to reinforce its reputation for competence while developing that more ambitious sense of economic purpose. That purpose is to lay the foundations for the knowledge economy, to imbue the economic constitution of the new economy with the values of the centre-left.

· 3 ·

EQUALITY AND
THE SOCIAL INVESTMENT STATE
Anthony Giddens

Classical social democracy thought of wealth creation as almost incidental to its basic concerns with economic security and redistribution. Neoliberals placed competitiveness and wealth generation much more to the forefront. Third Way politics also gives very strong emphasis to these qualities, which have an urgent importance given the nature of the global marketplace. They will not be developed, however, if individuals are left to sink or swim in an economic whirlpool. Government has an essential role to play in investing in the human resources and infrastructure needed to drive an entrepreneurial culture.

Third Way politics advocates a new mixed economy. Two different versions of the old mixed economy existed. One involved a separation between state and private sectors, but with a good deal of industry in public hands. The other was and is the social market. In each of these, markets are kept largely subordinate to government. The new mixed economy looks instead for a synergy between public and private sectors, utilising the dynamism of markets but with the public interest in mind. It involves a balance between regulation and deregulation, on a transnational as well as national and local levels; and a balance between the economic and the non-economic life of society.

A high rate of business formation and dissolution is characteristic of a dynamic economy. This flux is not compatible with a society where taken-for-granted habits dominate, including those generated by welfare systems. Social democrats have to shift the relationship between risk and security involved in the welfare state, to develop a society of 'responsible risk takers' in the spheres of government, business enterprise and labour markets. People need protection when things go wrong, but also the material and moral capabilities to move through major periods of transition in their lives.

The issue of equality needs to be thought through carefully. Equality and individual liberty can come into conflict, and it is no good pretending that equality, pluralism and economic dynamism are always compatible. Driven as it is by structural changes, expanding inequality is not easy to combat.

Social democrats should not accept, however, that high levels of inequality are functional for economic prosperity, or that they are inevitable. We should move away from what has sometimes in the past been an obsession with inequality, as well as rethink what equality is. Equality must contribute to diversity, not stand in its way.

For reasons I shall give below, redistribution must not disappear from the agenda of social democracy. But recent discussion among social democrats has quite rightly shifted the emphasis towards the 'redistribution of possibilities'. The cultivation of human potential should as far as possible replace 'after the event' redistribution.

The meaning of equality

Many suggest that the only model of equality today should be equality of opportunity, or meritocracy – that is, the neoliberal model. It is important to be clear why this position is not tenable. In the first place (were it achievable), a radically meritocratic society would create deep inequalities of outcome, which would threaten social cohesion. Consider, for example, the winner-take-all phenomenon, a demonstrable effect in labour markets. Someone who is only marginally more talented than another person may command a large salary difference from the other. A top tennis player or opera singer earns vastly more than one who isn't quite so good, and this happens not in spite of, but because of, the fact that a meritocratic principle is in operation. When barely perceptible margins make the difference between product success or failure, the stakes are enormous. Individuals perceived to make this marginal difference are rewarded disproportionately.

Unless it goes along with a structural change in the distribution of jobs – which by definition can only be transitory – a meritocratic society would also have a great deal of downward mobility. Many must move down for others to move up. Yet as much research has shown, widespread downward mobility has socially dislocating consequences and produces feelings of alienation among those affected. Large-scale downward mobility would be as threatening to social cohesion as the existence of a disaffected class of the excluded. In fact, a full meritocracy would create an extreme example of such a class, a class of untouchables. For not only would groups of people be at the bottom, they would be told that their lack of ability made this right and proper: it is hard to imagine anything more dispiriting.

In any case, a fully meritocratic society is not only unrealisable, it is a self-contradictory idea. A meritocratic society is likely to be highly unequal on the level of outcome. In such a social order, the privileged are bound to be able to confer advantages on their children – thus destroying meritocracy. After all, even in the relatively egalitarian Soviet-style societies, where wealth could not secure the advancement of children, privileged groups were able to transmit advantages to their offspring.

These observations do not imply that meritocratic principles are irrelevant to equality, but they do mean that they cannot be exhaustive of it, or be used to define it. How then should equality be defined? The new politics defines equality as inclusion and inequality as exclusion, although these terms need some spelling out. Inclusion refers in its broadest sense to citizenship, to the civil and political rights and obligations that every member of a society should have, not just formally, but as a reality of their lives. It also refers to opportunities and to involvement in public space. In a society where work remains central to self-esteem and standard of living, access to work is one main context of opportunity. Education is another, and would be so even if it were not so important for the employment possibilities to which it is relevant.

Two forms of exclusion are becoming marked in contemporary societies. One is the exclusion of those at the bottom, cut off from the mainstream of opportunities society has to offer. At the top is voluntary exclusion, the 'revolt of the elites': a withdrawal from public institutions on the part of more affluent groups, who choose to live separately from the rest of the society. Privileged groups start to live in fortress communities, and pull out from public education and public health systems. Inclusion and exclusion have become important concepts for analysing and responding to inequality because of changes affecting the class structure of the industrial countries. A quarter of a century ago a majority of the working population was in manual jobs, mostly in manufacture. Today, less than 20 per cent of the workforce in most of the developed economies is in manufacture, and the proportion is continuing to fall.

Some traditional working class communities have been revitalised, while others have sunk into decline. Like depressed inner city neighbourhoods, they have become isolated from the wider society. Where there is a strong presence of minority groups, ethnic prejudice can further reinforce exclusionary processes. As American cities long have done, cities in Europe are drawing in large numbers of immigrants, creating a 'new poor' in London, Paris, Berlin, Rome and other urban areas. Economic exclusion is thus often also physical and cultural. In declining areas, housing falls into disrepair, and lack of job opportunities produces education disincentives, leading to social instability and disorganisation. More than 60 per cent of tenants on a string of council estates around the City of London, the richest square mile in Britain, are unemployed. Yet City Airport, very close by, cannot find enough skilled workers for its needs.

Exclusion is not about gradations of inequality, but mechanisms that act to detach groups of people from the social mainstream. At the top, voluntary exclusion is driven by a diversity of factors. Having the economic means to pull out of the wider society is the necessary condition, but never the whole explanation, as to why groups choose to do so. Exclusion at the top is not only just as threatening for public space, or common solidarity, as exclusion at the bottom, it is causally linked to it. That the two go together is easily seen from the more extreme examples that have developed in some countries of the world, such as Brazil or South Africa. Limiting the voluntary exclusion of the elites is central to creating a more inclusive society at the bottom.

Many suggest the accumulation of privilege at the top is unstoppable. Income inequalities seem to be rising across a wide front. In the US, for example, 60 per cent of income gains over the period from 1980 to 1990 went to the top 1 per cent of the population, while the real income of the poorest 25 per cent has remained static more or less for 30 years. The UK shows similar trends in less extreme form. The gap between the highest-paid and lowest-paid workers is greater than it has been for at least 50 years. From 1980 to 1990, 42 per cent of income gains accrued to the richest 1 per cent. The lowest 25 per cent received 33 per cent of national income in 1979. In 1994 that proportion was 25 per cent. While the large majority of the working population are better off in real terms than they were twenty years ago, the poorest 10 per cent have seen their real incomes decline.

Yet it does not follow that such trends are set to continue or worsen. Technological innovation is imponderable and it is possible at some point the trend towards greater inequality might shift the other way. These trends are in any case more complicated than appears at first sight. As measured by some of the most exhaustive studies, income inequality has gone down rather than up in some developed countries over the past 30 years. Of course, we do not know exactly how reliable income data are – attempts to measure the secondary economy are guesswork. The secondary economy may worsen inequality, but it is more likely to act the other way, because informal economic activities – barter and unofficial cash transactions – are normally more common among poorer groups. Finally, those countries having a lengthy period of neoliberal government have shown higher increases in economic inequality than others, with the US, New Zealand and the UK leading the way.

Writing in relation to the US, the political journalist Mickey Kaus has suggested a distinction between 'economic liberalism' and 'civic liberalism'. The gap between rich and poor will keep growing and no one can stop it. The public realm, however, can be rebuilt through 'civic liberalism'. Kaus is surely right to argue that the emptying of public space can be reversed, and that tackling social exclusion at the top is not only an economic issue. Yet economic inequalities are certainly not irrelevant to exclusionary mechanisms and we do not have to give up on reducing them.

In the context of Europe, one key element is sustaining levels of welfare spending. The welfare state might stand in need of radical reform, but welfare systems do and should influence resource distribution. Other strategies can also be contemplated, some of them capable of wide application, such as employee stock ownership schemes, the redistributive implications of which might be substantial. A basic influence upon the distribution of income is growing sexual equality. Here income inequality is decreasing, not increasing, contradicting again the simple statement that society is becoming more unequal. Changes in the family affect structures of inequality. Thus in the UK in 1994–95, half of those in the top 20 per cent of incomes were either single full-time workers or couples both working full-time. The new patterns of inequality are not just given. They can be influenced by government policy, such as policies that support the involvement of single parents in the labour force.

'Civic liberalism' – the recapturing of public space – nonetheless must be a basic part of an inclusive society at the top. How can it be renewed or sustained? The successful cultivation of the cosmopolitan nation is one way. People who feel themselves members of a national community are likely to acknowledge a commitment to others within it. The development of a responsible business ethos is also relevant. In terms of social solidarity, the most important groups are not only the new corporate rich but also the members of the professional and monied middle class, since they are closest to the dividing lines which threaten to pull away from public space. Improving the quality of public education, sustaining a well-resourced health service, promoting safe public amenities and controlling levels of crime are all important. It is for these reasons that reform of the welfare state should not reduce it to a safety net. Only a welfare system that benefits most of the population will generate a common morality of citizenship. Where 'welfare' assumes only a negative connotation, and is targeted largely to the poor, as has tended to happen in the US, the results are divisive.

The United States has a higher level of economic inequality than any other industrial country. Yet even in that society, the homeland of competitive individualism, there is cause for hope that the 'revolt of the elites' can be contained. In his recent research, the sociologist Alan Wolfe found little evidence that upper middle class people were seceding from the wider society. He discovered broad-based support in America for social justice, 'as likely to be shared by conservative Christians as by East Coast liberals.' Most believe economic inequality in the US is getting too extreme:

> 'Economists who espouse a *laisser faire* approach to their discipline have been inclined to argue that high CEO salaries, even when seemingly outrageous, benefit everyone eventually, since inefficient companies or underpaid executives serve no one's real interests. But from the perspective of middle class America, high corporate salaries are more likely to be viewed as selfish, and selfish people and organisations, because they are out of balance, threaten the delicacy of the social order.'

It isn't difficult to think of policies that will have a positive effect on public space rather than corroding it. Health care, for example, should correspond to the needs of a wide constituency. 'Health care' here should be taken in a wide sense, commensurate with the idea of positive welfare to be discussed later. The reduction of environmental pollution, for example, benefits everyone. Indeed ecological strategies are a core element of lifestyle bargains, since most ecological benefits cut across classes.

Like social exclusion at the top, exclusion at the bottom tends to be self-reproducing. Any strategies which break poverty cycles should be pursued. As the Commission on Social Justice states:

> 'It is ... absolutely essential to help adults without basic skills or qualifications to acquire them, to help people whose skills are out of date to update them, and to raise the confidence of anyone whose morale has been undermined by a long period away from employment. People without skills are five times more likely to become unemployed than those with higher educational level qualifications; in the end employment goes to the employable.'

Education and training have become the new mantra for social democratic politicians. The need for improved education skills and skills training is apparent in most industrial countries, particularly so far as poorer groups are concerned. Who could gainsay that a well-educated population is desirable for any society? Investment in education is an imperative of government today, a key basis of the 'redistribution of possibilities'. Yet the idea that education can reduce inequalities in a direct way should be regarded with some scepticism. A great deal of comparative research, in the US and Europe, demonstrates that education tends to reflect wider economic inequalities and these have to be tackled at source.

Involvement in the labour force, and not just in dead-end jobs, is plainly vital to attacking involuntary exclusion. Work has multiple benefits: it generates income for the individual, a sense of stability and direction in life, and creates wealth for the overall society. Yet inclusion must stretch well beyond work, not only because there are many people at any one time not able to be in the labour force, but because a society too dominated by the work ethic would be a thoroughly unattractive place in which to live. An inclusive society must provide for the basic needs of those who cannot work, and must recognise the wider diversity of goals life has to offer.

Traditional poverty programmes need to be replaced with community-focused approaches, which permit more democratic participation as well as being more effective. Community building emphases support networks, self-help and the cultivation of social capital as means to generate economic renewal in low-income neighbourhoods. Fighting poverty requires an injection of economic resources, but applied to support local initiative. Leaving people mired on benefits tends to exclude them from the social mainstream. Reducing benefits to force individuals into work pushes them into already crowded low-wage labour markets. Community building initiatives concentrate upon the multiple problems individuals and families face, including job quality, health and child care, education and transportation.

A SOCIETY OF POSITIVE WELFARE

No issue has polarised left and right more profoundly in recent years than the welfare state, extolled on the one side and excoriated on the other. What became 'the welfare state', (a term not in widespread use until the 1960s and one William Beveridge, the architect of the British welfare state, thoroughly disliked) has in fact a chequered history. Its origins were far removed from the ideals of the left – indeed it was created partly to dispel the socialist menace. The ruling groups who set up the social insurance system in Imperial Germany in the late nineteenth century despised laisser-faire economics as much as they did socialism. Yet Bismarck's model was copied by many countries. Beveridge visited Germany in 1907 in order to study it. The welfare state as it exists today in Europe was produced in and by war, as were so many aspects of national citizenship. The system Bismarck set up in Germany is usually taken as the classic form of the welfare state. Yet the welfare state in Germany has always had a complex network of third sector groups and associations that the authorities have depended on for putting welfare policies into practice. The aim is to help these to attain their social objectives. In areas such as child care, third sector groups have almost a monopoly on provision. The non-profit sector in Germany expanded rather than shrank as the welfare state grew.

Welfare states vary in the degree to which they incorporate or rely upon the third sector. In Holland, for instance, non-profit organisations are the main delivery system for social services, while in Sweden hardly any are used. In Belgium and Austria, like Germany, about half the social services are provided by non-profit groups.

The Dutch political scientist Kees van Kersbergen argues that 'one of the major insights of the contemporary debate [about the welfare state] is that to equate social democracy and the welfare state may have been a mistake.' He examines in detail the influence of Christian democracy upon the development of continental welfare systems and the social market. The Christian Democratic parties descended from the Catholic parties that were important between the wars in Germany, Holland, Austria and to a lesser degree France and Italy. The Catholic unionists saw socialism as the enemy and sought to outflank it on its own ground by stressing co-determination and class reconciliation. Ronald Reagan's view, expressed in 1981, that 'we have let government take away those things that were once ours to do voluntarily' finds a much earlier echo in Europe in the Catholic tradition. Church, family and friends are the main sources of social solidarity. The state should step in only when those institutions do not fully live up to their obligations.

Recognising the problematic history of the welfare state, Third Way politics should accept some of the criticisms made of it by the right. The welfare state is essentially undemocratic, depending as it does upon a top-down distribution of benefits. Its motive force is protection and care, but it does not give enough space to personal liberty. Some forms of welfare institution are bureaucratic, alienating and inefficient, and welfare benefits can create perverse consequences that undermine what they were designed to achieve. However, the new politics sees these problems not as a signal to dismantle the welfare state, but as part of the reason to reconstruct it.

The difficulties of the welfare state are only partly financial. In most Western societies, proportional expenditure on welfare systems has remained quite stable over the past ten years. In the UK, the share of GDP spent on the welfare state increased steadily for most of the century up to the late 1970s. Since that date it has stabilised, although the gross figures conceal changes in the distribution of spending and the sources of revenue. Expenditure on education as a percentage of GDP fell between 1975 to 1995 from 6.7 per cent to 5.2 per cent. Spending on the health service, however, rose over this period. In 1975, it was equivalent to 3.8 per cent of GDP. By 1995, it had risen to 5.7 per cent (a lower percentage then in most other industrial countries). As has happened elsewhere, spending on social security increased most. In 1973–74 it made up 8.2 per cent of GDP. This reached 11.4 per cent by 1995–96. Expenditure on social security went up by more than 100 per cent in real terms over the period. The main factors underlying the increase were high unemployment, a growth in the numbers of in-work poor and changes in demographic patterns, especially a growth in numbers of single parents and older people.

The large increase in social security spending is one of the main sources of attack on welfare systems by neoliberals, who see in it the widespread development of welfare dependency. They are surely correct to worry about the numbers of people who live off state benefits, but there is a more sophisticated way of looking at what is going on. Welfare prescriptions quite often become sub-optimal, or set up situations of moral hazard. The idea of moral hazard is widely used in discussions of risk in private insurance. Moral hazard exists when people use insurance protection to alter their behaviour, thereby redefining the risk for which they are insured. It is not so much that some forms of welfare provision create dependency cultures, as that people take rational advantage of opportunities offered. Benefits meant to counter unemployment, for instance, can actually produce unemployment if they are actively used as a shelter from the labour market.

Writing against the backdrop of the Swedish welfare system, the economist Assar Lindbeck notes that a strong humanitarian case can be made for generous support for people affected by unemployment, illness, disability or the other standard risks covered by the welfare state. The dilemma is that the higher the benefits the greater will be the chance of moral hazard, as well as fraud. He suggests that moral hazard tends to be greater in the long run than in shorter time periods. This is because in the longer term, social habits become built up which then define what is 'normal'. Serious benefit-dependency is then no longer even seen as such but simply becomes 'expected' behaviour. Once established, benefits have their own autonomy, regardless of whether or not they meet the purposes for which they were originally designed. As this happens, expectations become 'locked in' and interest groups entrenched. States that have tried to reform their pensions systems, for example, have met with concerted resistance. We should have our pensions because we are 'old' (at age 60 or 65), we have paid our dues (even if they do not cover the costs), other people before have had them, everyone looks forward to retirement and so forth. Yet such institutional stasis is in and of itself a reflection of the need for reform, for the welfare state needs to be as dynamic and responsive to wider social trends as any other sector of government.

Welfare reform is not easy to achieve, precisely because of the entrenched interests that welfare systems create. Yet the outline of a radical project for the welfare state can be sketched out quite readily.

The welfare state as indicated earlier is a pooling of risk rather than resources. As Peter Baldwin states, what has shaped the solidarity of social policy is that 'otherwise privileged groups discovered that they shared a common interest in reallocating risk with the disadvantaged.' However, the welfare state is not well geared up to cover new-style risks such as those concerning technological change, social exclusion or the accelerating pro-portion of one-parent households. These mismatches are of two kinds: where risks covered do not fit with needs, and where the wrong groups are protected.

Welfare reform should recognise the points about risk made earlier in the discussion: effective risk management (individual or collective) doesn't just mean minimising or protecting against risks, it means also harnessing the pos-itive or energetic side of risk and providing resources for risk-taking. Active risk-taking is recognised as inherent in entrepreneurial activity: the same applies to the labour force. Deciding to go to work and give up benefits, or taking a job in a particular industry, are risk-infused activities – but such risk-taking is often beneficial both to the individual and the wider society.

When Beveridge wrote his 'Social Insurance and Allied Services', in 1944, he famously declared war on Want, Disease, Ignorance, Squalor and Idleness. In other words, his focus was almost entirely negative. We should speak today of positive welfare, to which individuals themselves and other agencies besides government contribute – and which is functional for wealth creation. Welfare is not in essence an economic concept, but a psy-chic one, concerning as it does well-being. Economic benefits or advan-tages are therefore virtually never enough on their own to create it. Not only is welfare generated by many other contexts and influences than the welfare state, welfare institutions must be concerned with fostering psy-chological as well as economic benefits. Quite mundane examples can be given: counselling, for example, might sometimes be more helpful than direct economic support.

Although these propositions may sound remote from the down to earth concerns of welfare systems, there isn't a single area of welfare reform to which they are not relevant or which they do not help illuminate. The guide-line is investment in human capital wherever possible, rather than the direct provision of economic maintenance. In place of the welfare state we should put the social investment state, operating in the context of a positive welfare society.

The theme that the 'welfare state' should be replaced by the 'welfare society' has become a conventional one in the recent literature on welfare issues. Where these are not already well-represented, third sector agencies should play a greater part in providing welfare services. The top-down dispensation of benefits should cede place to more localised distribution systems. More generally, we should recognise that the reconstruction of welfare provision has to be integrated with programmes for the active development of civil society.

SOCIAL INVESTMENT STRATEGIES

Since the institutions and services ordinarily grouped together under the rubric of the welfare state are so many, I shall limit myself here to comments on social security. What would the social investment state aim for in terms of its social security systems? Let us take two basic areas: provision for old age and unemployment.

As regards old age, a radical perspective would suggest breaking out of the confines within which debate about pension payments is ordinarily carried on. Most industrial societies have ageing populations and this is a big problem, it is said, because of the pensions time-bomb. The pension commitments of some countries, such as Italy, Germany or Japan, are way beyond what can be afforded, even allowing for reasonable economic growth. If other societies, such as Britain, have to some extent avoided this difficulty, it is because they have actively reduced their state pension commitments – in Britain, for example, by indexing pensions to average prices rather than average earnings.

An adequate level of state-provided pension is a necessity. There is good reason also to support schemes of compulsory saving. In the UK, the effect of relating pension increases to prices rather than earnings, without other statutory provisions, is likely to leave many retirees impoverished. A man who is 50 in 1998 and leaves the labour market aged 65 will receive a government pension amounting to only 10 per cent of average male earnings. Many people do not have either occupational or private pensions. Other countries have come up with more effective strategies. Many examples of combined public–private sector funding of pensions exist, some of which are capable of generalisation. The Finnish system, for example, combines a state guaranteed basic minimum income and earnings related pensions with regulated private sector provision.

The interest of the pensions issue, however, stretches more broadly than the questions of who should pay, at what level and by what means. It should go along with rethinking what old age is and how changes in the wider society affect the position of older people. Positive welfare applies as much in this context as in any other: it isn't enough to think only in terms of economic benefits. Old age is a new-style risk masquerading as an old-style one. Ageing used to be more passive than it is now: the ageing body was simply something that had to be accepted. In the more active, reflexive society, ageing has become much more of an open process, on a physical as well as a psychic level. Becoming older presents at least as many opportunities as problems, both for individuals and for the wider social community.

The concept of a pension that begins at retirement age, and the label 'pensioner', were inventions of the welfare state. But not only do these not conform to the new realities of ageing, they are as clear a case of welfare dependency as one can find. They suggest incapacity and it is not surprising that for many people retirement leads to a loss of self-esteem. When retirement first fixed 'old age' at 60 or 65, the situation of older people was very different from now. In 1900, average life expectancy for a male aged twenty in England was only 62.

We should move towards abolishing fixed age of retirement, and we should regard older people as a resource rather than a problem. The category of pensioner will then cease to exist, because it is detachable from pensions as such: it makes no sense to lock up pension funds against reaching 'pensionable age'. People should be able to use such funds as they so wish – not only to leave the labour force at any age, but to finance education, or reduced working hours, when bringing up young children. Abolishing statutory retirement would probably be neutral in respect of labour market implications, given that individuals could give up work earlier as well as stay in work longer. The provisions won't as such help pay for pensions where a country has overstretched its future commitments. They are agnostic about what balance should be aimed for as regards public and private funding. Yet they do suggest there is scope for innovative thinking around the pensions issue.

A society that separates older people from the majority in a retirement ghetto cannot be called inclusive. The precept of philosophic conservatism applies here as elsewhere: old age should not be seen as a time of rights without responsibilities. Burke famously observed that 'society is a partnership not only between those who are living, but between those who are living, those who are dead and those who are to be born.'

What of unemployment? Does the goal of full employment mean anything any more? Is there a straight trade-off, as the neoliberals say, between employment and deregulated labour markets – contrasting the US 'jobs miracle' with Eurosclerosis? We should note first of all that no simple comparison between the 'US model' and the 'European model' is possible. As economist Stephen Nickell has shown, labour markets in Europe show great diversity. Over the period from 1983–96, there were large variations in unemployment rates in OECD Europe, ranging from 1.8 per cent in Switzerland to over 20 per cent in Spain. Thirty per cent of OECD countries over these years had average unemployment rates lower than the US. Those with the lowest rates are not noted for having the most deregulated labour markets (Austria, Portugal, Norway). The position of the Third Way should be that sweeping deregulation is not the answer. Welfare expenditure should remain at European rather than US levels, but be switched as far as possible towards human capital investment. Benefit systems should be reformed where they induce moral hazard, and a more active risk-taking attitude encouraged, wherever possible through incentives, but where necessary by legal obligations. Since no one can say whether or not global capitalism will in future generate sufficient work, it would be foolish to proceed as though it will. Is the 'active redistribution' of work possible without counterproductive consequences? Probably not in the form of limits to the working week fixed by government – the difficulties with such schemes are well known. But seen in a wider context we have no need to ask whether redistribution of work is possible. It is already happening on a widespread basis, and the point is to foster its positive aspects. One much-quoted experiment is that at Hewlett-Packard's plant in Grenoble. The plant is kept open on a 24 hour cycle, seven days a week. The employees have a working week averaging just over 30 hours, but receive the same wages as when they were working a 37,5 hour week. Labour productivity has increased substantially.

Since the revival of civic culture is a basic ambition of the Third Way, the active involvement of government in the social economy makes sense. Indeed some have presented the choice before us in stark terms given the problematic status of full employment – either greater participation in the social economy or face the growth of 'outlaw cultures'. The possibilities are many, including time dollar schemes, and shadow wages – tax breaks for hours worked in the social economy. As a diversity of studies across Europe shows, 'more and more people are looking both for meaningful work and opportunities for commitment outside of work. If society can upgrade and reward such commitment and put it on a level with gainful employment, it can create both individual identity and social cohesion.'

In sum, what would a radically reformed welfare state – the social investment state in the positive welfare society – look like? Expenditure on welfare, understood as positive welfare, will neither be wholly generated by, nor distributed through, the state but by the state working in combination with other agencies, including business. The welfare society here is not just the nation, but stretches above and below it. Control of environmental pollution, for example, can never be a matter for national government alone but it is certainly directly relevant to welfare. In the positive welfare society, the contract between individual and government shifts, since autonomy and the development of self – the medium of expanding individual responsibility – become the prime focus. Welfare in this basic sense concerns the rich as well as the poor.

Positive welfare would replace each of Beveridge's negatives with a positive: in place of Want, autonomy; not Disease but active health; instead of Ignorance, education, as a continuing part of life; rather than Squalor, well being; and in place of Idleness, initiative.

This essay is adapted from *The Third Way* by Anthony Giddens, published by Polity Press.

NOTES

Baldwin P, 1990, *The Politics of Social Solidarity*, Cambridge University Press, Cambridge.

Beck U, 1997, 'Capitalism without work', *Dissent*, Winter 1997.

Burke E, 1910, *Reflections on Revolution in France*, Dent, London.

Callahan D, 1987, *Setting Limits*, Simon & Schuster, New York.

Commission on Social Justice, *Social Justice:Strategies for national renewal*, Vintage, London, 1994.

Fleming S, 1998. 'What we'll learn when we're 64', *New Statesman*, 5 June 1998.

Glennerster H and Hills J, eds, 1998, *The State of Welfare*, Oxford University Press, Oxford.

Hutton W, 1995, *The State We're In*, Cape, London.

Kaus M, 1992, *The End of Equality*, Basic Books, New York.

van Kersbergen K, 1995, *Social Capitalism*, Routledge, London.

Lasch C, 1995, *The Revolt of the Elites*, Norton, New York.

Lindbeck A, 1995, 'The end of the middle way?', *American Economic Review*, vol 85.

Nickell S, 1997, 'Unemployment and labour market rigidities', *Journal of Economic Perspectives*, vol 11.

Power A, 1997, *Estates on the Edge*, Macmillan, Baskingstoke.

Rifkin J, 1995, *The End of Work*, Putman, New York.

Timmins N, 1996, *The Five Giants*, Fontana, London.

Walsh J, 1996, *Stories of Renewal: Community Building and the Future of Urban America*, Report to the Rockfeller Foundation, New York.

Wolfe A, 1998, *One Nation, After All*, Viking, New York.

RETHINKING RETIREMENT

Ian Hargreaves and Ian Christie

AN AGE OF AGE

Summing up the twentieth century in a phrase is about to become a growth industry as we near the Millennium. A definition that underlines a key feature of modern social evolution is this: this century has been 'the age of age'. Every society has recognised people's changing maturity over their lifetime. Shakespeare famously delineated man's life into seven ages. But in our century people's precise age has gained unprecedented legal and cultural importance. This chapter explores some of the consequences for the future of welfare, and suggests that we need to rethink our approaches to retirement in the light of the changing meaning of age and changes in the life-cycles of millions of citizens.[1]

Age defines many of our greatest rights and responsibilities: to vote, to education, to work, to aspects of welfare and health care. We give people free education until the age of eighteen, the right to vote after that age, extra help with training and starting a career until the age of 25, and so on. At the other end of life we give women over 60 and men over 65 a host of old age benefits and no longer expect them to work. The exemption of under 21s from the minimum wage and increase in income support for the over 60s are only the most recent examples of a century-long trend.

In the past many of these rights were largely dependent on gender, wealth, title or perceived desert. Today, age is just about the only criterion on which discrimination is acceptable. And small anomalies in age-based rights generate enormous resentment. Think of the pressure to equalise the age of consent or harmonise regional guidelines on fertility treatment.

Awareness of specific ages pervades our culture. Adrian Mole – aged 13 and three-quarters – is not alone in his precise dating of his development. Consider how often we describe others by reference to their age. And for many of us, birthdays are our most important ceremonies, and the source of some of our greatest anxieties about our progress in life.

This 'coming of age' has many advantages. As a basis for judgements and distribution, age is a great equaliser. It recognises no gender, wealth or title. And age-based rights are rooted in practical considerations – the relative immaturity of the young and the relative infirmity of the old – not ideological preference. Using age as a proxy for need has been an efficient mechanism for distributing resources across our mass market for public support – it avoids the need for costly and divisive individual assessments.

But the significance and usefulness of age in this way has probably reached its zenith. Gradually its appropriateness as a marker of maturity, wealth and health is diminishing, eroded by changing patterns of work, education, family formation and health care. Improvements in nutrition, living conditions and medicine mean that many people stay healthier for longer. Developments in the economy and nature of work mean that formal education is often needed throughout life. Advances in reproductive technology mean that women have far more control over when to have children. Shifts in people's values have led to more variable patterns of relationships, including a spread in the age of first marriage and a rise in the number of second marriages.

The consequences of those changing patterns of life are pertinent to a host of public services. Sometimes the actual ages at which rights are given need to be re-examined. Sometimes age is no longer an appropriate marker of need at all. The education system is facing up to the demands for lifelong learning by introducing individual learning accounts. The justice system is reconsidering how it treats teenagers. And the National Health Service is struggling with new guidelines for fertility treatment. But it is our traditional system of welfare for the elderly which now seems most out of line with the emerging patterns of life.

RETIREMENT AGE

In our 'age of age', the retirement mark of 60 for women and 65 for men is second only to the age of majority in its legal significance. Reaching retirement entitles people to a higher income from the state, less tax, fewer health charges (for prescriptions and eye tests) and frequently a range of other benefits such as cheap public transport. On the downside, employees over 65 have no statutory rights and frequently face discrimination.

It is easy to see why the standardised retirement age has become so important. Firstly, it is a proxy for need. Societies have always supported the infirm. In our universal welfare system providing support to everyone over a certain age is an easy way to do that. Secondly, it allows a sufficiently long period of working in which to save for a few years not working before death. Thirdly, retirement itself is – to put it crudely – a handy way for employers to get rid of workers who are no longer quite up to their jobs. But evidence is accumulating that the current state retirement age is doing more harm than good.

Firstly, the age of 60 or 65 no longer seems a good proxy for need. Surveys suggest that although there are some near-universal needs among the retired – for instance, 97 per cent of over-65s need glasses or contact lenses – there is a large proportion of reasonably healthy, active and mobile pensioners. Over-65s make only two visits more to their doctor on average each year than do sixteen to 44 year-olds. And only about two out of every five pensioners report having any sort of disability. Far fewer are actually registered as disabled.

Proxies for need always risk some misallocation of resources. But considering the evidence that there are great variations in health and activity among the elderly, and the fact that the Government spends £67 billion pounds a year on pensions and other benefits to pensioners, the scope for misplaced spending based on the state retirement age is too big to ignore.

Secondly, retirement no longer represents just a sliver of years at the end of working life spanning nearly half a century. For many, work now starts considerably later than sixteen, the starting point assumed in the design of the original basic state pension system. For instance, the number of eighteen year-olds in full-time education has doubled in the last ten years.

Nor does work typically continue right up to the state retirement age any more. A quarter of men aged between 55 and 60 and over half of men aged 60 to 65 are outside the labour force. That means that they are not even looking for work if they are unemployed.

In short, a declining number of working years must support a gradually lengthening retirement. Today, the typical 65 year old still has sixteen years to live if they are a man, eighteen years if a women. By 2031 we expect those lengths of retirement to have risen to eighteen and 22 years respectively. The combined effect of these trends is that whereas retirement was once typically equivalent to less than a fifth of working life, today it often represents nearly half the working lifetime.

Given such tilting scales of working life and retirement, it is little wonder that many people fail to save enough for anything approaching a good life in retirement. According to one recent survey, two out of every five workers are heading for an income in retirement of less than 40 per cent of their final salary. Surveys of household expenditure show the consequences. When people retire they have to cut back expenditure on even basics such as food.

Thirdly, many older people find the transition to retirement extremely difficult. A life of leisure may seem appealing to the hard-pressed worker. But

most guides for retirement strongly advise readers not to 'retire' in any physical or mental way. As one America adviser recently put it, 'most people –
especially those who have been busy earlier in life – make the transition to
retirement if, and only if, they stay busy'. The Government's recent enthusiasm for supporting volunteering among the elderly is partly a recognition of
this.

Given these doubts about the usefulness of retirement at 60 or 65, at least
for many, it is surprising that the state has often reinforced these or other
lower ages. The age of retirement for women is due to rise to 65 by 2010.
But when personal pensions were introduced a decade ago the legislation
allowed them to be drawn from 50. And the public sector has been at the
forefront of moves towards retiring people long before 65. Often schemes
permit the use of early retirement from the age of 50.

Although the present government says it will combat age discrimination up
to the state retirement age, the message for those over 60 or 65 still seems to
be that they are different category of citizen. Income support for those over
60 increased by an extra £5 this year, on top of last year's winter fuel bonus.

AGELESS WELFARE
Taken together, these factors highlight retirement policy as one of our most
glaring collective failures: the state spends more than half the welfare budget on aged-based pensions entitlements, often giving money to healthy
people, yet most pensioners are still poor and by most accounts retirement
does little for their well-being. Indeed, often they would be physically and
mentally healthier if they kept at least some formal activity in their lives.

Designing an alternative policy is hard. After all, our attachment to the significance of specific ages is cultural as well as legal. A first step could be to
consider two principles which should inform a new approach:

1. Redistribution of resources should be made on the basis of people's
    need and abilities to work rather than age alone.
2. If people choose to save for a period of retirement at the end of their
    life, that should be no more or less privileged than saving for other peri-
    ods of out of paid work, such as retraining, bringing up children or sim-
    ply a period of refreshment from a strenuous career.

The case for redefining redistribution criteria
The amount of money redistributed on the basis of age, rather than disability, is difficult to calculate. The basic state pension – which costs £30 billion
a year – combines redistribution and insurance in one system. Separating the

redistributive element is impossible, but it is certainly large. Income support, council tax benefit and housing benefit payments to pensioners, which are all purely redistributive, cost £9 billion a year. But probably more of these recipients are infirm compared to the pensioner population as a whole, and recipients would still receive lower benefits if old age criteria were removed. Redistribution also takes place to the better off through the pension system. Up to a quarter of a pension can be taken tax free, at a cost of £2 billion to the Government in lost revenue. And pensioners start paying tax at a higher income than those of working age.

Although a precise level of redistribution on the basis solely of age – not disability – is therefore difficult to assess, the scale of these expenditures suggests that such redistribution is enormous, given that three out of five pensioners are not disabled. Freeing such resources would allow significantly more to be given to the poor, sick and disabled elderly who need the money most.

The case for ending the privileges for individual pension provision

Of course, moving away from age as a basis for redistribution should not mean that individuals could no longer retire. Many might decide to use their own savings for such a purpose. But at the moment few people have a choice about retirement. Age is the only criterion on which employers can dismiss someone without being open to a legal challenge – workers over 65 have no employment rights. Many are lucky if they can even stay that long, or find another job in their late forties or fifties if they are made redundant. Survey research indicates that four out of five citizens believe employers discriminate against older people.

Nor is an alternative pattern of working less intensively during a longer working life financially attractive. Comparatively, pension contributions enjoy far greater tax privileges than saving for retraining, bringing up children or simply taking a year or two out of an increasingly pressured workplace. And people are compelled to make some contributions to a pension scheme in any case.

But there is considerable evidence that breaks from working are as necessary as eventual retirement is. The hours at work for those in employment have been creeping up over the last decade. So has reported work-related stress. With over four out of five full-time working women claiming that they never have enough time to get everything done (up from three out of five a decade ago), surely we should try to design a system which gives at least equal weight to spreading work over the lifetime as it does to squeezing it into a few decades followed by decades of retirement.

TOMORROW'S POLITICS

Redistributing to the old on the basis of infirmity, not just age, and treating retirement by the healthy in same way as any other period outside the labour force would change our welfare system profoundly. So we should proceed slowly and cautiously with changes. After all, most of us are planning our lives around the current system. And, as noted earlier, using age as a proxy for need has been an easy way to distribute resources. Simply replacing it with the current system of supporting the sick and disabled could be a disaster.

The redesign of welfare to meet the new demographic and socioeconomic realities is at an early stage and no one has ready answers to the problems it poses. But two essential ingredients are clear: providing employment opportunities for older people and innovations in support for individuals as they develop new patterns of working and saving.

Employment

Before support for healthy elderly people is in any way reduced, some large changes are needed in the labour market to allow those over 65 to achieve a greater income from earning. At the moment, all the change is in the wrong direction: the proportion of income which pensioners get from paid employment has been declining for decades.

The Labour government's declared aim to reduce age discrimination in the workplace is welcome. At the moment they believe that voluntary action will be enough: 'When a quarter of the workforce is over 50 a few years hence employers will no longer be able to ignore older workers' is the standard justification. That argument would be more convincing if we forgot that employers have managed to discriminate on the basis of gender for centuries despite half of those of working age being women. The evidence from tackling other forms of discrimination suggests that voluntarism will not be enough.

A first step should be to ensure that age in itself is no longer a legal basis for dismissal. In the United States, such legislation is already in place. Alongside that, legislation covering age discrimination in recruitment and conditions is likely to be necessary.

The state will also need help those many organisations that are simply not equipped to manage older people – who often have less energy for manual work or the full-time 'long hours culture' which pervades many workplaces, but who are nonetheless able to do useful work. A number of organisations are already making the changes – such as Tesco and B&Q – but others will need support to make a shift to a new workplace culture. Some of

that help should be in the form of advice and sharing best practice, both to
organisations and individual older people themselves. But there may also be
a need for short-term subsidies to encourage companies to take on older
workers and hence change their working practices. At the moment older
workers are often perceived as expensive to hire because their pension entitlements are high.

Advice and empowerment in dealing with saving
The second precondition for change is a new system of support. Before
being cast adrift from the old structure of working life and retirement, to surf
the waves of retraining, parental leave, refreshment breaks, part-time working in old age and so on, most of us will want some guidance and resources
to equip ourselves to thrive in the world of new life-cycles.

One of the advantages of the current system is that it provides a structure
in which individuals, employers, the state and financial service companies
all have a role. However much pension provision is inadequate for twenty
years of retirement, saving for retirement is still more successful than saving
for other needs such as a period of retraining. Half the population have less
than £500 in any form of saving account, National Saving or stocks and
shares. Removing the existing structures of pension support and advice without introducing alternatives could lead to confusion and inappropriate financial decisions, as the scandal of personal pension mis-selling demonstrates
all too clearly.

Because people's financial needs are more variable as the life-cycle
changes, the structures for supporting saving in the twenty-first century will
need to be less of a 'one-solution-fits-all' nature. But they need not be less
inclusive. The Health Service is a good example of a system which deals
with greatly varying needs, but is still universal. As with health care, people
partly need to be helped to develop their own ability to look after themselves financially – that is why financial education in schools would be an
important foundation for supporting a new system of welfare. People will
also need sound advice. Often that advice can be general, provided through
information and benchmarking certain types of product. Occasionally it
needs to be personal, which the Government should consider supporting
through subsidies for financial 'health checks' from an accredited advisor
every decade or two.

Perhaps the greatest challenge for the state will be supporting other organisations which help people manage their resources over a less predictable
life-cycle. Already a few employers are allowing people to choose which
benefits they receive – longer holidays, a higher pension, child care vouch-

ers and so on. Small mutual organisations can also offer people a structure for lifetime financial planning. Such organisations can be supported, at the very least, with a simple regulatory and legal structure. They could also be given financial assistance.

Shifting resources and privileges away from certain ages and towards assessment of needs

Provided work were available for older people and people had the ability to plan and save for their own provision in old age, or at any other period of their life, then the state could start shifting resources away from supporting retirement on the basis of age alone. That would be a very complex process, for most of us have built up rights and expectations under the current system. Those rights would need to be protected.

A starting point could be to gradually equalise the tax regime for retirement provision and for provision for other breaks from work. That could be achieved by bringing pensions into line with the current tax regime for other savings – taxing income when it is earned – or allowing more saving under a pension-like tax system – paying no tax on income that is saved and instead paying it when the savings are drawn down. All saving could be covered under such a system if the Government were prepared to suffer a drop in income tax receipts.

Secondly, age-related benefits, such as the pensioner premium for income support and basic pension, could be held constant and the age on which those benefits were payable could be gradually increased. The resources saved could be redirected to the poor and infirm.

Allocating such resources would be difficult. The state's approach to assessing disability and ability to work has often served both individual claimants and taxpayers poorly. With the number of people claiming incapacity benefits trebling over the past two decades, the Government already needs better ways of assessing ability to work. We are learning that effective welfare assessments need to be made by those who know the recipient well. The introduction of single advisers/assessors for all benefits is a helpful first step in that process.

As resources allocated to people on the basis of age gradually declined, so too could compulsory pension contributions. The greatest argument for compulsion is that without it people would unnecessarily rely on aged-based rights, such as income support, when they could have afforded to save for their own old age provision. If these were lower, compulsory pension contributions could be lowered too. In a new system, compulsory insurance for sickness and disability would need to rise, but probably not to the same extent as pension contributions could fall, freeing people to save more of their resources as they choose.

THE POLITICAL CHOICES

The measures sketched out above are just an outline of the sort of policies that are likely to be appropriate for tomorrow's system of welfare. They indicate the enormity of the changes required. The temptation will be to do nothing. But gradually the do-nothing option appears less and less tenable. Already unease is growing over age discrimination in the workforce and over the demands on people simultaneously to work long hours, learn new skills, bring up children and save for retirement during the traditional 'working life'. And even with our current system, many people make inadequate provision for a decent quality of life in retirement or for long-term care. Bluntly, the current system is not working.

So tomorrow's politicians face a choice. They can either try to ensure that an increasing number of healthy elderly people enjoy a decent retirement by raising compulsory pension contributions and increasing rights and saving privileges on the yardstick of age, or they can start moving towards and alternative, less age-based policy. The first would require considerably more resources, the second a radical change in benefits, workplaces and public expectations. In between lies drift – rhetoric about support for pensioners and assurances that everything will be fine, while in reality more of both the healthy and infirm elderly become impoverished. Aspiring politicians, please take note.

NOTES
1. This essay draws heavily on previous analysis of retirement by Ben Jupp, a Senior Researcher at Demos, including *Saving Sense: A new approach to encourage saving*, Demos, London, 1997, and *Reasonable Force: The place of compulsion in securing adequate pensions*, Demos, London, 1998.

5

PROBLEM-SOLVING GOVERNMENT

Perri 6

For 50 years, the British public, whenever asked, has consistently reported the same four top priorities for the governments it elects. We want government to reduce crime, ill-health, poor educational achievement and unemployment. That small job done, we are prepared to worry about pensions, the environment and other pressing problems.[1]

Over the post-war period, reported and unreported acquisitive and property crime has risen steadily, with the largest increases being for car crime. Unemployment has fluctuated wildly but for a generation has been counted in the millions. Health has improved for everyone, but the inequalities in health between the classes have not; and longevity brings its own new health challenges. Educational achievement has risen overall, but there remains an embarrassingly long tail of failure, and the relevance of even the best education for the practicalities of adult life in the new century is not always obvious.

Moreover, government costs us more in absolute terms than ever before. In twenty years of effort, no British administration has succeeded in getting the bill for government below two-fifths of national wealth. As a result, government is usually unpopular. On the other hand, the public remains attached to the principle that public action is needed to tackle the big problems: if anything, the public is more, not less, convinced of the need for public action that it was both ten and twenty years ago.[2] In short, the voters have hardly got what they wanted, still less at a price they are prepared to pay. The same rock and hard place can be found wrapped around governments in most of the developed world.

One response is to point to all the things that cause crime, unemployment, poor educational attainment, accidents and disease, and to argue that there is little more than government could practically or affordably do about them. On this view, government should stop raising people's expectations and get out of the business of trying to solve social problems. People can do better left alone. Some go further and argue that any government powerful enough to make a real impact on these problems would be tyrannical: the cure is worse than the disease, and the public has greater liberty under government that lacks the means to solve complex, 'wicked' social problems.

Another view is that if only the voters would be prepared to put up with higher taxes, government could throw more money at these problems and tackle them effectively. What is needed, on this view, is 'one more heave'.

But both the 'get out of this business' argument and 'one more heave' theory are unconvincing. The voters, understandably, refuse to put up with the fatalistic view that public action is unable to confront large social evils. The arguments from some sections of the Conservative Party in recent years for scaling back civilian government[3] did not dent the British citizen's view that public action could, at least in principle, be effective in these areas.

On the other hand, after such a long record of disappointment, no one can seriously argue that it will be enough simply to put more cash into the machinery of executive government departments and agencies, local authorities and quangos and the clusters of businesses and voluntary agencies providing public services under contract. Since the public sector no longer runs these services exclusively, but depends on networks of private and non-profit providers, the time has come to speak of the 'public interest services' than the 'public services'.[4] But whatever we call the arrangements, after a decade of contracting out public services, it will require more than just parcelling out existing services to other organisations to make real impact on crime, ill-health, unemployment and poor educational achievement.

No one can offer a political strategy and a reform of government that can credibly guarantee that the great evils of crime, illness, ignorance, idleness, want and environmental damage can be solved once-for-all, still less guarantee to do all this for less than two-fifths of national wealth. Nor is the purpose of this essay to offer such snake oil.

But there are things that can be done. Even if we do not have full solutions, we know something about the forces that over the long run cause these evils, and we have learned something from efforts in many countries, about what works – at least up to a point – and what does not. And we know something about the flaws in our system of executive government that need to be fixed if any progress is to be made. While expectations may continue to rise beyond our capacity to meet them, government does not have to perform so badly as it currently does. Indeed, there is every reason for optimism. Faced with a challenge, organisations in any sector can rise to it. Just as the British private retail sector learned to make huge improvements in service and quality standards during the 1980s, so the public sector learned remarkably how to make the reforms of the 1980s and early 1990s work, and can boast some inspiring examples of learning and public entrepreneurship.[5]

This essay sets out the elements of a strategy for rethinking the goals of executive government, its organisation and its relationship with citizens, which, I will argue, offers the best chance currently available for governments in the developed world to get out from between the rock of high public expectations and the hard place of their reluctance to pay higher taxes, by improving, not the efficiency, but the *effectiveness* of what government does.

The basic elements of the strategy are: shifting the balance of effort across government from trying to cure or relieve harms when they have already happened; integrating the accountability, financing, organisation of services around outcomes rather than activities, functions or professions; and putting as much on persuading public to think, believe, care and behave differently as on delivering services.[6] These are fundamental changes, and they require us to think differently about ethics in government. After setting out this agenda, the essay concludes with arguments about political ethics of this new direction for government.

GETTING RETALIATION IN EARLY

Most of what government does is to intervene after people have suffered harm, either in an attempt to cure the problem or at least to relieve the worst symptoms. With one large and one small exception, just a tiny proportion of what government does is designed principally to prevent harms from occurring in the first place. The large exception is education, which has – for most of those who succeed in it – a preventive effect upon unemployment. The small exception is the combination of diplomacy and military spending, which can be used to prevent wars occurring. But the capacity of the education system to prevent educational *failure* is patchy and weak, however measured (indeed, it is hardly ever measured properly – a sign of priorities). Our schools still leave a section of the population destined for marginal employment.

Elsewhere prevention is a low priority. Less than 2 per cent of what is spent on criminal justice is devoted to preventing crime. Similarly slim proportions of what is spent on medicine go to preventing disease and accidents.This might not matter so much if the effort put into cure and palliative care worked well. But it does not. Fewer than one in five procedures in regular use in conventional medicine has been shown to be clinically effective in a majority of cases. The clear-up rates of crimes from detection are low, amounting to a small proportion of crimes reported, and a tiny proportion of those committed. Cleaning up after pollution is famously difficult to do effectively, and government does it badly. Benefits may or may not trap many people into long-term unemployment, but the evidence of 'churn' into and out of low-paid and low-skilled jobs in the bottom two income deciles suggests that even the combination of benefits, vocational training, advice, and tough incentives is failing to do much for the employability of the poorest.

More than this, *only* preventive action *could* be effective against many of these evils. For cures work usually only with one set of causes, and great evils have many causes. The real sources of disease are to be found in diet, exercise, housing and working conditions, water quality, personal health-related behaviour, air quality and other environmental factors. By contrast, advances in medicine explain only five years of the total increase in life expectancy in the twentieth century.[7] Any preventive strategy for health would have to work across all these areas and focus on the many sources of disease, accident and injury. Similarly, the roots of crime are in cultures of aspiration, poor or neglectful parenting, educational failure, poverty, social neglect. No amount of detection, punishment or even deterrence could tackle these things. The same can clearly be argued for educational failure, unemployment and environmental damage.

But do we know enough about how to do effective prevention to scale up the effort? And if we did, can we be confident that, later on, we could as a result make savings in the budgets for curative and palliative government?

In fact, much more is known about effective prevention than is being used. There have been some striking successes in preventive health policy in the twentieth century, with regulation of housing and working conditions, air and water quality, food standards, and with the combination of tax disincentives and persistent information about the risks of smoking and drinking alcohol. In recent years, a series of local initiatives using combinations of targeted information and judiciously modest public spending on encouragement to use facilities have shown that improvements in diet, hygiene, exercise and kitchen safety can be achieved cost-effectively by comparison with the curative approach. The costs of preventive work on educational failure – from remedial teaching to basic literacy classes and targeted teenage years intervention on truancy – are eventually recouped many times over in taxes paid that would not otherwise have been. Community crime prevention is certainly a complex business, but there are innovations and experiments that have proven much more cost-effective than detection and punishment, bringing together design improvements, family support, educational efforts, new housing management practices, and other interventions.[8]

The periods of time over which effective preventive programmes work varies greatly. Some community crime prevention initiatives can produce measurable results in the form of lower rates of crime within a few months. On the other hand, early years nursery, play and pre-school education pro- grammes may only show their results in the form of reduced truanting, drug use and crime many years later. Public health initiatives also vary in the timescale of their effects. Intensive programmes to improve dietary under- standing and practice can, when targeted at the least knowledgeable parents, show results in child health within a few years. But fluoridation of drinking water, while yielding dramatic reductions in dental disease, takes years to show benefits.

It is sometimes argued that elected governments must be 'short-termist', and therefore preventive programmes that take years to produce results will not be supported on anything other than a marginal scale. But evidence for this gloomy claim is not impressive. In fact, it has been the *most* democrati- cally responsive societies in the developed world – the USA, Switzerland and Sweden – that have the most advanced public health and crime prevention programmes. Indeed, there is strong and durable opinion poll evidence in Britain that early years support, water fluoridation and vaccination pro- grammes are generally very popular.

Moreover, British governments have been able to undertake long-term programmes in many areas. For example, anti-discrimination laws were introduced in the 1960s and 1970s that were not particularly popular at the time and did not really show results until ten years later, by which time they had become accepted and even popular; major anti-smoking initiatives that did not show major results for almost a generation have been undertaken and widely accepted; tax incentives for the take up of private pension schemes were introduced in the 1980s that were only beginning to yield results when, ten years later, they were scaled back, having achieved the desired kickstart for the market. Of course, there are plenty of cases where governments will focus on immediate results and only measure those aspects of performance that will show short-term variations – such as school league tables.

Apart from doubts about cost-effectiveness, the usual objections of princi- ple to scaling up the preventive role of government are concerned with fears of excessive public power. Some fear that prevention will mean the intrusive 'nanny state' poking into every aspect of our private affairs, paternalistically manipulating our lifestyles in what it deems to be our best interests. Clearly, not everything that might be both preventive and effective would be acceptable, and some guidelines have to be enforced against the enthusiasm or malice of officials. But the same has long been true for the control of curative interventions: it is simply that these controls are now second nature, and no longer seem so salient. The charge of paternalism is one to which I return in the final section.

But a deeper reason why we do not do more prevention concerns a particular conception of justice which has become allied with professional power. The idea that justice consists in providing responses to certain types of needs that have already arisen has deep roots in humanitarian ethics. Nor would anyone argue that the impulse is misguided, at least as an account of human *virtue*. However, as an account of the *priorities of justice*, the 'insurance for cure' model produces strange results. It seems to lead to the argument that justice consists in waiting until harms have befallen those most at risk, before intervention is warranted on ground of justice. If we know in advance who is most likely to be at risk, this seems manifestly unfair. Now that we know more about how to conduct cost-effective prevention, we need to develop a richer conception of preventive justice.

The great professions that have grown up to administer curative and palliative work – medicine, policing, social work – have enormous vested interests. By contrast, the preventive professions – trading standards enforcement, environmental health inspection, public health promotion – are much weaker, sometimes trapped within curative professions (directors of public health must be medical doctors first). In many fields – community-based crime prevention, for example – no profession exists to bring together all the activities involved.

Most importantly, the curative professions of medicine and policing have often been able to secure public support for the claim that their work should take priority. They can appeal to generous humanitarian instincts, can display heroic interventions under great pressure, and their work makes good TV documentaries or drama. The humdrum business of preventing things from happening has, by definition, only the absence of drama and misery to show for its best results. Only occasionally is the averting of disaster capable of stirring the emotions – for example, when an epidemic is stopped or a notorious neighbourhood is visibly turned around in a few short years. Our Victorian forebears, who took preventive health so seriously that they invented local government to implement it, would surely be distressed to hear our politicians actually boast that they spend more of the taxpayers' money every year on curative health care. They at least knew failure when they saw it.

Of course, government cannot get out of the business of cure and relief completely, and even where it can, the process will be slow. Detection,

imprisonment, accident and emergency provision, and surgery will doubt-
less be with government as long as taxes are. People will rightly demand
that some emergency support be available on a curative basis. We cannot
prevent all harms to health. In the end we all need some palliative care,
although with luck we shall be able to reduce the unavoidable period of
ill-health at the end of life for many people. Nor would a society that
sought to prevent all kinds of harm be a particularly inspiring one in which
to live.

However, in order to finance increased preventive effort in those areas
where it is just, necessary and appropriate that the taxpayer should support
some activity, there are many curative and palliative services that it might be
reasonable to ask people to finance individually or as households, rather
than collectively. For example, where people want health care procedures
whose effectiveness falls below some democratically agreed threshold, perhaps there is a case for phasing in – probably over long periods of time for
younger cohorts – a withdrawal of NHS insurance and encouragement to
take out private insurance or savings products. The standard objection to
such a transition is that, as with pension reform, 'the young pay twice – once
privately for themselves and once publicly for the old'. However, where people are being expected to take more responsibility for curative and palliative
services, they have an incentive to reduce their burden by making greater
use of prevention. Moreover, there are ways of temporarily reducing the burden for the transition cohorts, if we are prepared to be imaginative, for
example, by offering them partially offsetting income tax reductions, especially for the least well-off.

Joining up

Two defining characteristics of the great evils that the public elects governments to tackle are that they cannot effectively be combated on a curative
basis, nor can they be combated by the work of any one profession or function of government. Only when many services are brought together is there
a reasonable prospect of success.

But great professions have grown up within the structures of government
into the silos and chimneys which are the functional departments of state,
local government and quangos. Indeed, the last generation of reforms in
public management were designed in ways that exacerbated this problem.
The creation of 'single-minded' agencies that would 'focus like a laser beam'[9]
on the carrying out of one or two specific activities, subject to a battery of
performance measures expressed almost exclusively in terms of the volumes
of activity and the cost, has exacerbated some old problems in the public

sector of poor coordination and the dumping of tough cases between agencies. So, equipped with 'management focus' under the crudest version of league table competition, schools exclude the most difficult pupils and load the costs upon the criminal justice system, and, focused upon health care or social care only, the NHS and local authority social services play a squalid game of 'pass the parcel' with frail elderly people.[10]

Not only is this wasteful, it has reinforced exactly the wrong kind of accountability in the public interest services. Accountability for activity and simple cost-efficiency is simply not adequate if what citizens want from public interest services is that they achieve certain outcomes, namely, *reduction* in the great social evils. Since no single functionally defined and organised agency can have direct administrative control over any outcome, the challenge for the new generation of public management reform is to create *systems of accountability for outcomes that cut across as many functional boundaries as the problems do*. This idea, which runs contrary to traditional ideas of public management but which is at the heart of contemporary ideas of 'community governance', is central to the agenda of what I have called 'holistic government'. Holistic government is about integration of the accountability of functions, professions, resources, inputs to outcomes.

The toolkit for integration is only now being developed. One instrument that has proven effective in some settings is holistic budgeting. Here, a single budget is attached to the achievement of an outcome – urban regeneration, say, or crime reduction – and the purchaser has the power and duty to buy across functional boundaries. There have been some successes with experiments such as the Single Regeneration Budget. Less ambitiously, dumping by agencies can be penalised by charging them the costs of the problems they dump, on the model of environmental pricing of polluting practices.

The development of smart purchasing more generally needs to accompany these kinds of strategies. The public sector needs to build up a high status cadre of purchasers who will be independent of the traditional professions, who can think imaginatively about the design and purchase of cross-professional packages, often cheaper packages, and wherever possible preventive packages of effective services.

Holistic government or, in the prime minister's preferred phrases, 'joined-up government' and 'joined-up solutions', has already become part of the rhetoric of public managers and local and national politicians. This is important: seizing the commanding heights of the vocabulary is a vital step, for their own language can be quoted back at politicians and officials, when they fail to live up to it. Improving the quality of hypocrisy is always the first stage of major reform.

However, it is only the first. Too often the emphasis has not been on genuinely holistic action focused on achievement and measurement of outcomes. Rather, much of the effort has been concentrated on partnerships
between agencies – local councils, health authorities, Training and Enterprise
Councils and so on – which involve costly negotiations. These often yield
only pooled 'to do' lists expressed in terms of activity and resources, or of
vague goals rather than outcomes. Indeed, there may be ways in which
holistic budgets, holistic information systems and accountability for outcomes can be used to by-pass the need for putting so much management
time into solving partnership problems, and instead purchasing packages
from agencies and professions that will require them to find ways to work
together in any case. In any case, this will require much more effort in the
design and use of outcome measurement systems, and the development of
smarter purchasing.

But most importantly, most experiments with holistic government have yet
to take the preventive agenda seriously. Holistic service design on the curative model has an important place in the repertoire, but the real challenge is
to achieve the outcomes the public wants without excessive taxation. The
next phase in the holistic government agenda must be *the development of
mainstream budgets around outcomes at the local level*, with incentives to
choose preventive strategies wherever possible. Secondly, we need to develop outcome-based systems of auditing to supplement and eventually encom-
pass simple value-for-money auditing of activities.

The open persuader

Unemployment, ill-health, poor educational achievement, crime and environmental damage can only be prevented and tackled effectively if we are
prepared to find ways of persuading people to think, care, believe, hope and
behave differently – in short, if we can change the cultures, not so much of
the government bureaucracy or the businesses that work for government,
but of key segments of the public. The last generation of government
reformers too often imagined that with tax and benefit incentives, they could
target and change behaviour directly, without having to work through cultures. This was misguided. Despite ever higher taxes on nicotine, alcohol
and petrol, ever sharper disincentives for unemployed people to remain on
benefits and heavier fines for petty offences, there remain significant problems of health, unemployment and crime. Moreover, incentives can be costly to administer, and they are subject to the law of diminishing returns. But
most importantly, human motivation is much more complex than the simple
hydraulics of economic incentives recognise.[11]

It is important to try to change attitudes and aspirations. For example, for many unemployed people the simple comparison between income tomorrow from an available job and income tomorrow from a combination of job-seekers' allowance and housing benefit shows a net loss from working. At first sight, this seems a simple matter of badly designed incentives. In fact, the real issue is the cultural one of the level of aspiration and the time horizon over which the returns to the initial loss of income from working are calculated, when taken together with opportunities for training on the job and the improved employability from the curriculum vitae and the new contacts made through work. Actually, for most people over the economic cycle, poorly paid jobs are stepping stones, not dead ends.[12] But making a poorly paid job into a stepping stone requires motivation, aspiration and a willingness to make calculations over longer time horizons. There is little of this in current government offers to unemployed people.

Similarly, unless cultures of parental involvement in school, of neighbourliness, of waste recycling and so on are addressed, no (affordable) amount of financial incentives will change behaviour sufficiently to improve educational performance, reduce crime or reduce environmental damage from pollution and over-use of resources.

It is often the 'weak' tools of government – education, training, information, persuasion, praise and blame, leadership, symbolic action, example-setting – which are most cost-effective in efforts to influence cultural change. For example, the success achieved – recognising recent setbacks – in combating smoking has been as much the result of information and persuasion about health risks as of the tax disincentives or prohibitions on smoking. As life expectancy increased, many of those who fatalistically thought that they would probably die of something else by the time that smoking wrecked their health have come to recognise that they can hope for longer life, and that avoiding cigarettes is worthwhile.

Similarly, improvements in diet and exercise are as much the result of influencing demand as of consumer protection law or the provision of leisure facilities. And the symbolic effects of the regulation of equal opportunities between men and women, and of outlawing racial discrimination, have surely played a much greater role in the change in attitudes on these issues in Britain and other countries since the 1960s, than any deterrent effect from the infrequent and not always successful law enforcement by the equality commissions.

Cultural change is about working on willingness to effect, not merely ability to afford, certain changes in behaviour. That is why it is both essential and, when designed well, effective.

THE ETHICS OF PROBLEM-SOLVING GOVERNMENT

A central objection to holistic government is that the agenda is paternalistic. Services such as many hospital surgical procedures, or police officers on the beat, are popular with voters, while preventive services may not be. Even if something is more effective, critics on both left and right argue, it is paternalistic to favour services deemed by experts to be in the interests of the populace. Moreover, people have come to trust in the fragmented, silo-based government they have inherited, because particular professions have successful 'brands': for the 'nanny state' to seek to persuade us to change our aspirations, values, motivations and cultures in our own better interests is unacceptably paternalistic, the critics argue. The job of the state is to take the citizenry, both individually and collectively, as they are, and respond democratically to their preferences about collectively financed services as well as their individual preferences when dealing with them singly, whatever experts think about it.

These charges deserve an answer. The problem with the general antipaternalist argument is that it makes almost any kind of governance impossible. Modern complex societies cannot be run either wholly on what majorities will support, or by restricting the individual's encounter with the state to a pick-and-choose relationship. However, it could not be right that government may do anything at all that would be effective in pursuit of our best interests. It must be constrained in certain ways. Acceptable paternalism must surely, in a liberal democracy, be limited, constrained and accountable.

There are, I will argue, three basic building blocks on which such limits and accountability must be built. The first is a very specific principle of implied consent. It is true that the public is sometimes attached to particular activities or inputs that are not effective. If we are to offer holistic services that are more effective in pursuit of health, low crime, employability and better learning, then we need strong justifications for overriding those preferences and specific limitations on the conditions in which it can be done.

A good basic test of implied consent to the overriding of preferences about the current activities of government is to ask whether the public also has preferences about the outcomes that it wants government to pursue that are: a) settled – have been evident priorities for long periods; b) fundamental – appear to be foundations on which much of other public opinion is based; c) expressed basically in outcome terms; and d) clearly priorities for action.

If there are such preferences – and my reading of the public opinion data on the priority of tackling crime, illness, ignorance and joblessness is that there are – then there is a case for overriding preferences about activities, providing other safeguards are in place, and only in ways that are otherwise acceptable (do not violate rights, and so on). Only in something akin to an emergency can we justify overriding majority preferences where these conditions are not met. The challenge for the environmentalists who wish to override public love of car-driving, when the public attaches a lower priority to environmental outcomes, is to make out the case that the consequences of failure do so will lead to environmental emergency.[13]

The second building block is an argument about democratic delegation. While some regard governments as merely the slaves of current majority popular will, this is in practice nearly always set aside in democracies. Implicitly, we delegate to governments a power and duty to enquire into the causes of great evils and the best means of combating them, and a power and duty to act upon those findings. Without this, it is hard to make sense of the powers that make government possible at all.

Thirdly, the government that does override current preferences must be accountable to the voters for doing so. Indeed, one can argue that the more it does so, the more accountable it must become. Therefore, the more it innovates in ways that might run counter to majority views, the more it must be innovative in explaining itself to the public and in giving citizens ways to play a part in decision-making and comment on the results achieved.

The defence for limited paternalism is analogous. No modern democracy can function without both responding to the cultures of the sovereign people (Tom Paine) and attempting to influence at least some of them (Edmund Burke). The justification for choosing to influence cultures must be in the public's own settled priorities for problems that it wants solved. The means by which it overrides preference must not violate rights: therefore the presumption must be that wherever possible, the weak tools of government should be used for changing cultures, and the strong tools resorted to sparingly.

If this argument is accepted, it would justify pushing ahead with more preventive programmes in health promotion and crime prevention, more holistic budgeting in social policy, even at the expense of additional resources for the National Health Service or additional police on the beat, provided that certain other things are done. First, it must monitor effectiveness and publish the results: charters, published league tables and comparisons between prevention and cure should be central to government information policy. Secondly, it must provide greater opportunities for local referenda and deliberative polling and other opportunities for participation in decision-making about deployment of resources.

Finally, the integration of government highlights old concerns about privacy. For many people, privacy was best protected by the inefficiency of

government and its inability to pool information. In the new era, governments will have to be much more innovative in demonstrating that privacy
is protected by codes of ethical practice for personal information. It will be
important to develop a code of practice for the whole of the public services,
that is as holistic as data flows are, providing citizens with much more detail
on the information ethics of every tier of government than the principles in
the data protection legislation currently do.[14]

TOMORROW'S GOVERNMENT

The central problem for government is, and has been for some decades, to
achieve more in its domestic agenda, with no increase in the proportion of
national wealth to pay for that greater effectiveness. While some European
countries such as Germany and Sweden and France have hitherto sustained
larger proportions of their national wealth going through the state, this is
proving increasingly costly, and in any case, there are sharper constraints in
Britain upon what levels of taxation are acceptable to voters, at least without very significant improvements in outcomes first, that may not apply in
countries with deeper, more widespread and more enduring social democratic sensibilities than are found in Britain. Unable – rightly – to increase its
share of the cake, therefore, government must on the one hand try to ensure
that the economy delivers a bigger cake in absolute terms, and on the other,
it must re-think how it pursues its goals. The last generation's solution to this
problem was the 'reinvention of government' (or 'the new public management'). That era is coming to an end, as it runs out of problems that its prin-
cipal tools – dedicated agencies, measurement of activities and costs, financial incentives, continued priority for cure and palliation – are well-equipped
to solve.

A new approach has begun to emerge in the 1990s, which offers the best
hope currently on the horizon for resolving that central difficulty. The full
shape of the new era is only beginning to emerge, but three central strands
will be prevention, integration and the use of weak tools for cultural change.
It is one of the ironies of history that this optimistic agenda has emerged at
a time when the policy professionals in universities, consultancy firms and
newspapers are in a trough of fatalism about the prospects for government
reform. Among the chatterati, the talk is all of unintended consequences, the
impossibility of changing cultures, the veto power of the professions and the
policy networks, the rigidity of budgets and the failures of previous reforms.
It is too early to say that the Cassandras will be proven wrong, but there are
good reasons for optimism. We know more about the toolkit for preventive,
holistic and culture-changing government than ever before, and the skills are

becoming more widely diffused. The public is better informed about risks and opportunities through the media than ever before.

Moreover, this is a field in which Britain has a comparative advantage over the rest of the developed world, Having been the first to enter the 'reinventing government' phase in the early 1980s, it was first out in the early 1990s, and is now ahead of many North American, antipodean and European states at least in designing holistic systems of governance, although it still has much to learn from the rest of the world about prevention.

Government has been charged by the voters with some key priorities, and has secured a share of national resources and legal powers that no other institution can hope for. It has assembled a body of knowledge of 'what works' that is at least as good as that available to business for its challenges. For too long, government has lacked confidence, ambition and imagination about how these goals can be achieved. The twenty-first century could be one in which government begins actually to solve problems. Which is what it is for in the first place.

NOTES

1. MORI, monthly, British public opinion, MORI, London: see questions 'What would you say is the most important issue facing Britain today?' and 'What do you see as other important issues facing Britain today?'. Responses to these questions are not prompted. See also Jowell R et al, annually, *British social attitudes*, Dartmouth Publishing, Aldershot, which includes questions on priorities for public spending.

2. See note 1 (Jowell et al).

3. See for example, Duncan A and Hobson D, 1995, *Saturn's children: how the state devours liberty, prosperity and virtue*, Sinclair Stevenson, London.

4. 6 P, 1998, 'Ownership and the new politics of the public interest services', *Political Quarterly*.

5. See, for example, Leadbeater C and Goss S, 1998, *Civic entrepreneurship*, Demos, London.

6. This strategy is set out in more detail in 6 P, 1997, *Holistic government*, Demos, London.

7. Bunker JP, Frazier HS and Mosteller F, 1994, 'Improving health: measuring the effects of medical care', *Milbank Quarterly*, vol 72, 225-258, summarised in Tarlov AR, 1996, 'Social determinants of health: the sociobiological transition', in Blane D, Brunner E and Wilkinson R, eds, 1996, *Health and social organisation: towards a health policy for the twenty first century*, Routledge, London, 71-93; Wilkinson R, 1996, 'How can secular improvements in life expectancy be explained?' in Blane D, Brunner E and Wilkinson R, eds, 1996, *Health and social organisation: towards a health policy for the twenty first century*, Routledge, London, 109-122.

8. Bright J, 1997, *Turning the tide: crime, community and prevention*, Demos, London.

9. These phrases were Rt Hon Michael Heseltine's from 1982, announcing the first Urban Development Corporations.

10. Leat D and 6 P, 1997, *Holding back the years: how Britain can grow old better in the twenty first century*, Demos, London.

11. 6 P, 1997, 'Governing by cultures', in Mulgan G, ed, 1997, *Life after politics: new thinking for the twenty first century*, HarperCollins, London.

12. OECD, 1996, *The OECD jobs study*, 3 vols, OECD, Paris.

13. See Christie I, 'Ecopolis: Tomorrow's politics of the environment', this volume.

14. 6 P, 1998, *The future of privacy, vol 1: private life and public policy*, Demos, London

A STEP BEYOND MORRIS DANCING: THE THIRD SECTOR REVIVAL

Ian Hargreaves

When Margaret Thatcher became Prime Minister in 1979, she had a strong instinctive sense that an inefficient public sector needed to be transformed by the power of market forces. What she lacked was a clear idea of how to achieve her goal. The manifesto on which she fought the 1979 election thus gave little clue to the scope of a privatisation programme which would have far-reaching effects not only in Britain but also, when emulated, throughout the world.

This essay suggests that Tony Blair is in a comparable situation. Having articulated a powerful, instinctive rhetoric about community and partnership between the public, private and third (non-profit) sectors of the economy, he must now, in office, construct a programme to deliver it.[1] That means releasing the potential of the third sector, the least developed of the partners in this new mixed economy. It is the only alternative to either a retreat to big government or excessive reliance upon big business.

The argument here is not that the third sector should be boosted or given privileges by virtue of some innate moral superiority, but that it is an essential and currently underperforming part of the economic and social mix. To prosper, like the private sector, it needs a fair and sympathetic legal and economic framework. The extent to which, beyond that, non-profit groups receive financial privileges ought to depend upon the extent to which they deliver, in an efficient manner, social goods. There is, however, good reason to believe that the third sector is particularly well placed to tackle those multi-dimensional 'wicked problems', such as entrenched poverty, drug abuse and chronic educational under-achievement, which are high on the political agenda but which have defied the skills of the public sector and do not interest the private sector. Already, the third sector dominates social housing, since Thatcherism's retreat from council housing, and it has played a crucial part in developing many new services, such as pre-school education. But it is wrong to think of the third sector as confined only to the more obvious social services; through the BBC, for example, it dominates an otherwise commercial broadcasting industry. The central characteristic of the 'social economy' is that the goods it provides will not be supplied reliably without strong, positive regulation, and sometimes significant public expenditure.

But for all the current interest in the social economy, across continental Europe and the Americas, Britain's third sector remains small, stuck at an estimated 4 per cent of economic output.[2] We need to understand how to drive it forward, to make it a richer resource base in the ecology of our social and political institutions.

TELL SID: THIS IS THE BIG ONE

So what can New Labour learn from the experience of privatisation in the 1980s? The table below seeks to capture the main points of comparison, setting the context of the new Conservative government in 1979–80 and the private sector alongside the circumstances facing the present Labour government (operating in an unusual partnership with the Liberal Democrats) and the third sector now.

	PRIVATISATION	THIRD SECTOR
1. IS THERE A PROBLEM/CRISIS TO BE SOLVED?	YES	YES
2. IS THERE WIDESPREAD AGREEMENT THAT CURRENT APPROACHES ARE NOT ADEQUATE?	YES	YES
3. IS STRONG POLITICAL LEADERSHIP AVAILABLE?	YES	YES
4. IS THERE AN ENTRENCHED INTEREST TO ATTACK?	YES	YES
5. DOES THE IDEA HAVE GLOBAL POTENTIAL?	YES	YES
6. IS THERE AN ADEQUATE ALTERNATIVE INSTITUTIONAL MODEL AVAILABLE (E.G. PLC IN THE CASE OF PRIVATISATION, VERSUS STATE CORPORATION)?	YES	MAYBE
7. IS AN ADEQUATE REGULATORY APPROACH AVAILABLE?	MAYBE	MAYBE
8. CAN PERFORMANCE BE MEASURED AND ACCOUNTABILITY ESTABLISHED?	MAYBE	MAYBE
9. IS THERE A READY SOURCE OF CAPITAL?	YES	NO
10. IS THERE A FORCE OF POWERFUL SELF-INTEREST OUTSIDE GOVERNMENT WHICH CAN DRIVE THE PROCESS?	YES	NO

What this shows (points one to five) is that there is widespread agreement today that we face a set of problems (mostly the 'wicked problems') where the private sector does not see sufficient opportunity for commercial reward and to which the public sector is too risk-averse and insufficiently entrepreneurial to tackle. As in 1979, there is strong political leadership, plenty of entrenched interests to assail (in both the central and local state) and a lively potential for policy advance in this area to be picked up around the world, where similar problems abound.

Points six to eight, however, raise more awkward questions about the third sector. In comparison with the shareholder-owned company, which has survived centuries of change to emerge as the dominant institutional form of modern, global capitalism, the legal and institutional framework of charities (to take a substantial slice of the third sector) is highly problematic, to the point where there are widespread calls for the fundamental revision of charity law which dates from 1601, meeting government resistance on the grounds that such a revision would be too complex. It has also been suggested that charities face 'a crisis in confidence due to their increasingly commercial orientation, their close association with the public sector through the contract culture or negative press coverage.'[3] Meanwhile, the new government's Better Regulation Task Force has argued, simplistically, that voluntary groups are over-regulated. The politicians, it seems, do not know whether to retreat or wade deeper in specifying a framework for the third sector.

At the same time, there are palpable problems in what is left of Britain's mutual sector. In the financial services industry, mutual building societies are in retreat, not only in Britain but in Australia, South Africa and America, although some are fighting a belated rearguard action. The truth is that mutual building societies and insurance groups, not to mention retailers, have often provided inferior services than their plc competitors while being no better at being accountable to their owners. The point of rebuilding the third sector is not to attack profit-seeking, which has a vital economic function, and still less to endorse under-performance or to featherbed it with fiscal privilege. What we need to do is to ask the right questions about third sector organisations themselves and to establish to what extent their problems arise from an inadequate public policy framework.

Against these points of difficulty for the non-profit sector, however, it is also worth noting that when Mrs Thatcher set off down the road of privatisation, there was no regulatory model to guide her. It is also true that shareholder-owned companies also face challenging questions about their accountability to stakeholders – the legitimacy of their 'licence to operate' as it was called by the Royal Society of Arts in its Tomorrow's Company inquiry – and questions brought freshly into focus over the future of top football clubs like Manchester United – owned legally by shareholders, but subject, surely, to wider true ownership than that. The lesson of Thatcher's approach to privatisation is that sometimes it is necessary to act boldly without knowing all the answers in advance.

It is in points nine and ten of the table, however, that the hardest questions are addressed. The truth is that the third sector is chronically short of capital, especially of the patient, risk capital required for the construction of serious, sustained enterprises; this will never be delivered by profit-seeking markets alone.

Nor is there any obvious answer to point ten. Privatisation may have been an idea rooted in the analysis that nationalised industries were simply not capable of competing in world markets, but it gathered its unstoppable momentum from the markets. Whenever the political will for more privatisation flagged, the City drove it on. Clearly, the third sector has no 'Sid', no greed factor at work and its growth can only be propelled by altruism or at least a wider social purpose. Given the relatively healthy condition of Britain's civil society, however, with over 20 million people a year volunteering for some form of socially useful activity, this is not a make-or-break difficulty.[4] What it indicates is that the motivating force of a third sector revolution must be political, in its broadest sense, rather than financial.

CIVIL SOCIETY, COMMUNITY AND THE THIRD SECTOR

Some will draw a pessimistic conclusion from this analysis. The third sector, they will say, like the poor, is always with us. Why not let it meander along, at 4 per cent of GDP, responsible for somewhere between 400,000 to 950,000 jobs, with £15 billion to £30 billion a year in income – useful, but not vital?[5] The fact that it has not made a bigger breakthrough, in spite of its many privileges, indicates its unfitness.[6]

There are many reasons to resist such pessimism and not only because of the sense that we are bumping up hard against the limits to public trust in both the public and the market sectors.

There is not space here to rehearse in detail the arguments about the importance of civil society, as a place where citizens freely act together to consolidate and express their freedoms, to solve problems, to provide services to each other or simply to enjoy each other's company. Much of the recent impetus in this argument arose from analysis of the collapse of Soviet Communism, but it has fed into the mainstream of new centre-left thinking on both sides of the Atlantic.

EJ Dionne, the American political commentator, argued in a recent Brookings Institution volume[7] that

'the civil society debate is not a flash in the pan or a trendy effort to inject the appearance of life into a national debate that is failing to engage the country. The civil society idea is popular because it responds to problems inherent in other ideas. Its rise reflects three developments with deep roots.

'The first is a move among thinkers on both left and right to reflect on the failures of their respective sides and face evidence that may be inconvenient to their own arguments. The second is a widespread sense that changes in the economy and in the organisation of work, family and the neighbourhood have outpaced the capacity of older forms of civil and associational life to help individuals and communities cope with the change. The third is the impact of an anti-government mood that has been part of American life since the 1970s. The interest in civil society reflects both a reaction against government and a desire to reconstruct energetic government on stronger ground.'

It is important to note the distinction between this argument and the one made from the right during the 1990s by, for example, David Green, Director of the Health and Welfare Unit of the Institute for Economic Affairs, who has attacked the welfare state for eroding 'the sense of personal responsibility and mutual obligation on which a resilient civil society rests' and Thatcherism's 'market society [which] provides inadequately for the health and welfare of its citizens'.[8]

Green's position, that these errors will correct themselves if only the state draws back, is wrong. The centre-left position, articulated by Dionne (and by Blair and Clinton) is that a healthy civil society involves 'energetic government' at many different levels, local, regional, national and transnational. Anthony Giddens, in his book *The Third Way* (from which chapter three of this collection is extracted), argues that 'government can and must play a major part in renewing civic culture.'[9]

In the British context, this 'radical centre' position seeks to build upon a pre-Labourite tradition, valuing, in Blair's words, 'the contribution of Lloyd George, Beveridge and Keynes and not just Attlee, Bevan or Crosland'.[10] Gordon Brown said last year that the government could only achieve its goals 'in partnership with business and the voluntary sector' – the welfare-to-work programme has, in a limited way, put this into practice. 'The government's vision is, put simply, the recreation of a civic society', Jack Straw, the Home Secretary, told the National Neighbourhood Watch conference last year, and in his Geraldine Aves memorial lecture, Straw's deputy, Alun Michael, went back to John Stuart Mill for a classic defence of the principles involved:

> 'A people among whom there is no habit of spontaneous action for a collective interest – who look habitually to their government to command or prompt them in all matters of joint concern – who expect to have everything done form them – have their faculties only half developed ... It is of supreme importance that all classes of the community should have much to do for themselves; that as great a demand should be made upon their intelligence and virtue as it is in any respect equal to; that the government should encourage them to manage as many as possible of their joint concerns by voluntary cooperation.'[11]

In July this year, William Hague, the Conservative leader, warned that he would not allow Labour to monopolise the argument for an expanded civil domain, though his party's confusion about Europe, devolution and local government underscores the point that it is not possible to talk sense about civil society without taking a clear view on the essential role of the state, in all its manifestations.

John Kay, in arguing the merits of pragmatism in the Third Way – 'The big idea is that there is no big idea'[12] – identifies the fact that it is only within civil communities that shared values are preserved and, taking a well-aimed swipe at romantic communitarianism, suggests that businesses, the City, universities and accountancy partnerships are the most important communities of modern life, 'not troupes of Morris dancers or residents' associations'. The successful firm, says Kay, 'is one whose characteristics are well adapted to the environment in which it trades.'

But Kay's point is as easily applicable to not-for-profit groups like the BBC, housing associations, Oxfam, Greenpeace, the Bank of England (or indeed Morris dancers) as it is to Glaxo-Wellcome, the hybrid new London–Frankfurt stock market or the London School of Economics. These communities of interest require certain conditions to sustain them if their wider value is to be maximised, thus specifying a central objective of 'energetic government' policy towards the third sector: to ensure that those conditions exist. The third sector does not pretend to be the sole guardian of civil society's legitimate institutions, but in creating a zone for organisations whose purpose is social, rather than the pursuit of the maximum return for share-holders, it broadens our moral and social vision and gives us additional routes through which to address our problems.

In its turn, the third sector must acknowledge that it competes for cus-tomer loyalty and government backing against a business sector which is capable of great efficiency and dynamism (and which is becoming ever more sophisticated in its ability to adapt to the requirements of its environment) not to mention a public sector which is becoming more conscious of the need to pursue holistic approaches to solving problems. The inescapable conclusion is that all three sectors (public, private and third) have a great deal to learn from each other and that as they increasingly act in partnership together, we will wish to see the emergence of new hybrid forms of organ-isation, along with sustained networks of inter-action between players from the three sectors, using information technology, which will amount to much the same thing as the new hybrids. This is the way in which many institu-tional forms of the next twenty or 30 years will emerge.

These, then, are some of the reasons why there is a wide public interest in a thriving third sector:

- It is morally desirable for citizens to be able to express their instincts to help others, rather than contracting out all of these actions to 'profession-al' or 'state' services. Specifically, effective and affordable care of children and the elderly demands that a substantial level of responsibility be accept-ed within the family and the wider local community on a voluntary basis.
- The changing structure of employment and the distribution of time between the 'time squeezed' and the 'over-leisured' means that more peo-ple will mix activity in the formal and informal sectors of the economy. The third sector has played a hugely important role in generating jobs in France and Germany in recent years.[13] Many of the key policy priorities of the next years will depend upon the voluntary giving of time: literacy, numeracy, crime reduction and welfare-to-work all require an abundant supply of mentors.
- Community-level third sector organisations arise from a close understand-ing of local needs and are more likely to be able to negotiate permission to act and so pursue successful strategies than more remote external agen-cies. Examples include Neighbourhood Watch-type crime-prevention strategies, community-run parks and playgrounds, and services for drug abusers.
- Information technology makes possible new communities of interest and allows small-scale community organisations to network with each other

for purposes of learning and shared services.

- Mutual organisations are capable of conferring a sense of ownership, which in turn can promote higher ethical standards (such as resistance to fraud) than is the case with commercial firms (such as insurance companies) or the state (for example, the Benefits Agency.)
- Many third sector organisations, operating on a small scale and flexibly, are ideal for experiments in social provision. In areas like the environment and overseas aid, they have shown considerable powers of innovation: for example, Greenpeace, Oxfam and Amnesty International. On a smaller scale, there is increasing attention to the work of 'social entrepreneurs' and 'civic entrepreneurs' and their success in driving through on-the-ground solutions which have eluded the public sector and have not interested the private. Such organisations also have a flexibility, for example in employment and decision-taking structures, which is much harder for the public sector to adopt.[14]

WHAT IS TO BE DONE?

In spite of much rhetoric, no post-war British government has focused upon the task, identified by Jack Straw, of reinvigorating civil society. Post-Beveridge Labourism was suspicious of alternatives to state provision. One Nation Conservatism was complacent. Thatcherism, though it created space for the third sector by ordering the state to retreat from key functions and to concentrate upon purchase rather than service provision, lacked a positive strategy for the country's wider social well-being. It is the emergence of the state as regulator which creates dramatically increased scope for both the private and third sectors, but which in turn demands both a clear legal framework and a quality of accountability in the third sector which far exceeds current norms.

The legal framework and accountability

Almost every substantial analysis of charity or the third sector has reached the conclusion that charity law is dangerously outdated. The Deakin Report (The Commission on the Future of the Voluntary Sector) in 1996 called for 'a single, inclusive definition of charity, based on a new concept of public benefit.' Many charities sail perilously close to the legal wind in their political and trading activities and numerous third sector organisations engaged in vital public interest work in community-building and economic regeneration have found that they are better operating as companies limited by guarantee, rather than seeking charitable status. That creates obvious difficulties when they seek partnership funding from foundations, the general public or business.

The government has acknowledged that 'legal definitions ... are seriously overstretched', but has rejected as too complex and too demanding of parliamentary time the task of redrafting basic charity law. Instead, the Charity Commission has embarked upon an exercise termed a 'review of organisations on the register' and is consulting upon whether charities established to tackle unemployment and urban or rural regeneration can meet its 'public benefit' test. At the same time, the National Council for Voluntary Organisations has embarked upon a two-year study of charity law. These look like tentative first steps when the problem calls for bold strides.

What is needed is a robust, workable, legal definition of an independent, non-profit-distributing organisation, legitimately able to compete against private business and required to operate transparent rules of governance, in place of the current rules for trusteeship, which are primarily designed to avoid scandal and which often prevent the individuals who are the driving force of third sector organisations sitting on their own boards. In the words of an earlier Demos report: 'The time has come to question whether the constraint against the distribution of financial rewards for successful performance, in the world of community-based and mission-driven organisations, is particularly useful and, where it is useful, whether it should be combined with unlimited liability.'[15]

A healthy third sector would contain organisations able to amend their purposes according to contemporary need, rather than being the prisoners of ancient deeds of endowment, as too many are. This would also make it easier for third sector organisations to cease their activities, when they run out of energy, or to merge, as many should. Modern regulation would be based upon five elements:

- the quality and price of service to consumers
- economic regulation to ensure that competition is fair
- financial and personal integrity
- achieving core goals
- a strong culture of self-regulation.

Such regulation needs to occur at both national and local levels and involves a blend of policing by supervisory authority and self-regulation based upon agreed codes of practice (the Joseph Rowntree Foundation's proposed code of April 1997 contains most of the necessary elements in the latter category). In practice, much of the oversight would result from interaction between third sector organisations and the public and with organisations purchasing services – themselves often branches of government, including local government. (The desperate need to re-establish effective and self-confident local government, 'steering not rowing' lies outside the scope of this chapter, but it is essential to the future of the third sector.) Many areas in which the third sector is active will also involve sector-specific regulatory requirements – such as education, care for the elderly, pensions and housing. It scarcely needs to be said that the current regulatory approach, based upon the Charity Commission and primarily focused upon issues of financial integrity around a narrow definition of 'public benefit', is well and truly obsolete.

The right regulatory structure will work in the interests of transparency, rather than in the interests of the third sector *per se*. For example, when one potential supplier of the National Lottery service proposes a 'not for profit' game and a second proposes one involving return to shareholders, the public needs to know which proposal will reliably bring most benefit to good causes – it is the job of regulation to achieve that transparency. Without such transparency, it is impossible for the third sector to demonstrate its legitimate advantages. With proper regulation, it will be impossible for the third sector to conceal its inefficiencies.

Taxation and the availability of capital

Under existing law, charities are exempt from corporate and some other forms of taxation and most donors can increase the benefit of their gifts to their chosen charities through the use of devices such as covenants.

Since these financial benefits accrue only to organisations capable of claiming charitable status and since the definition of what constitutes charitable is seriously confused, the whole edifice of government financial support for the third sector rests upon the shakiest of foundations.

Without radical reform of charity law, it is difficult to see how progress can be made in better targeting fiscal incentives to the third sector. Such fiscal privileges will always be controversial, in that some private traders will argue that they are being unfairly discriminated against. But the principle of offering incentives for organisations that trade without distributing profit and within a regulatory framework which guarantees their integrity is robust. What is needed is a wider definition of what constitutes such an organisation, in order to allow for the inclusion of non-profit-distributing partnerships, mutual organisations, co-operatives and other forms of social enterprise. Credit unions, for example, which have filled an important gap in the provision of financial services to 'un-banked' communities, do not qualify for charitable status on present rules.

It is also important to recognise that there is a wide variety of ways in which commercial activities are subsidised, ranging from the provision of huge investment grants to foreign investors whose operations are expected to create jobs, to the fact that the Post Office, a public sector institution, in effect underpins the operation of thousands of village shops.

If we switch to a problem-solving perspective, rather than one based upon entrenched institutional positions, the picture becomes clearer. All communities need a basic minimum infrastructure of transport, shops, financial service (including access to benefits), medical service, policing and basic educational and child care facilities. If these are not provided spontaneously by the private sector or by the state, it makes sense to offer incentives for the third sector to fill the gap. It is difficult to see why the private sector, which has abandoned the provision of shops, banking and transport in thousands of communities, should be allowed to resist their efficient provision by appropriately well-founded community groups.

Only if these alarming legal anomalies are addressed is it possible to imagine government acquiring the confidence to invest more tax revenue in the third sector, or indeed to redistribute what it already provides. In the past twenty years, most Treasury initiatives have involved gimmicky attempts, mostly unsuccessful, to provide incentives for growth in charitable donations.

In short, the third sector must be taken seriously, not alternately featherbedded and patronised. Here are some of the ways in which that might be accomplished:

- To help the third sector generate investment capital, we need a UK-wide network of 'social capital banks', ideally operated in partnership between the private sector, government and the third sector, endowed with sufficient capital to provide loans and longer-term forms of investment against clear criteria concerning social objectives, as well as standards of efficiency and probity.[16] Funding for these banks could come from governments, the private sector (duly incentivised) and the release of 'trapped' capital resources inside some older charities (again, using incentives).
- To provide incentives for partnerships, including tax-beneficial arrangements for companies entering into partnerships to deliver public goods alongside third sector organisations.
- Incentives for volunteering, which could include accrual of entitlement to pensions and other insurance benefits for volunteers of the kind available to paid employees.
- Citizens' earmarking of taxes: allowing all taxpayers to denote on their tax returns a category of spending to which they would like to see, say, 1, 2

or 3 per cent of their income tax devoted. Alternatively, tax-payers could nominate specific, registered charities as recipients of such funding – so-called 'voluntary taxation.' This could operate at the level of local as well as national taxation.

- Endowment – the gift of capital and real estate through inheritance or other bequest – has provided the core financial strength of numerous charities over centuries. Government needs to shape incentives to attract such bequests to third sector organisations, especially at a time when greater longevity and the need to self-finance care in old age is under-cutting the market in inheritance. It also needs to help those charities that have accumulated huge capital surpluses that cannot sensibly be spent upon the charity's legally authorised functions, to release these funds for more productive purposes.

Technology

The emergence of relatively cheap communications technology, based around the Internet, has opened up new possibilities for third sector organisations to learn from each other, to share services, to debate problems, to raise their profile and to improve their transparency and accountability. The fact that many large businesses are delayering management hierarchies and using the same technology to develop networked, more entrepreneurial approaches should encourage the third sector to play to its strengths. Initiatives like the Community Action Network, which links social entrepreneurs, have brought together funding from the private and public sector, using an entrepreneurial style to build a new piece of public infrastructure.

A STEP BEYOND MORRIS DANCING

There has been a profusion of interest in the third sector in recent years, but there is a tendency still, in John Kay's words, to think of it as 'troupes of Morris dancers and residents' associations'.

Unless the third sector is trusted to play a significant part in areas of policy that are central to government's purpose, it will be seen as marginal. This means that, if the government is to be taken seriously, it must find ways of bringing the third sector into its reform of the welfare state, into health care and into education.

This is scarcely an outlandish idea, given the pre-welfare state role of friendly societies or the churches in education. It is entirely possible to imagine, say, a second pensions system (a successor the State Earnings Related Pensions Scheme, sometimes in government documents called a Stakeholder

Pension) run by mutually owned societies, in which members retain owner-ship of their own investments, but which is supported by taxpayer funds to enable the poorest to take part in the scheme. The issues of accountability and performance which arise with such a proposal are certainly no more daunting than those raised by the debauching by government of the National Insurance Fund, annexed as a part of general taxation, or the private sector failures revealed in the personal pensions mis-selling scandal.

In health, there is sufficient experience of community health centres to envisage community ownership of them; hybrid forms of ownership else-where in the health service will be essential, as they are in general practice and dentistry. The third sector is well placed to link provision of primary care with related public health and leisure facilities.

Equally, in education, it seems unlikely that parental ambitions will be sat-isfied without forms of non-profit mutual ownership of schools – a familiar model in other countries, such as Holland, Germany, the Scandinavian coun-tries and Hungary, where parents are allowed to 'claim' from the state the sum of money allocated to the education of their own children and to use the funds to set up new schools. Tom Bentley develops this argument in chapter six.

In his study of the welfare state Nicholas Timmins points out that when Margaret Thatcher was elected in 1979, she was surrounded by think tanks which had radical instincts about the welfare state, but which lacked con-crete understanding of the system, preventing them devising plausible reforms.[17] He quotes Oliver Letwin, an adviser to Thatcher in the Downing Street Policy Unit, as saying: 'there was plenty of intellect available. What there wasn't was knowledge.'

The current government has open access to the knowledge of a sympa-thetic third sector. It can boldly go where no modern predecessor has dared. At present, the signs are that it has sensed the potential, but lacks the will and clarity of thought to drive forward the radical legislative agenda, with-out which its instincts will come to nothing much. Given that the third sec-tor tradition has its roots as much in Burke and Mill as in Paine and the Rochdale Pioneers, it is worth bearing in mind that if Blair's Third Way can-not accommodate the third sector in tomorrow's politics, then perhaps some-one else's will. Don't tell that to Sid. Tell it to William.

NOTES

1. Blair, launching the revised Clause IV of the Labour Party in 1995, said the new wording 'puts our values of community, of social justice, democracy, equality, partnership, at the forefront.' In his first speech as prime minister, delivered on a South London housing estate, Blair said the new government would back 'thousands of social entrepreneurs, those people who bring to social problems the same enterprise and imagination that business entrepreneurs bring to wealth creation.'

2. The latest Dimensions of the Voluntary Sector report published by CAF in July 1998 suggests that the 500 largest charities have experienced rising income, but a Barclays/NGO Index notes the first quarterly fall in total income since its computations began in 1992. NCVO's research suggests that the number of people donating to charity has fallen by 20 per cent since 1993 (a phenomenon it connects with the arrival of the National Lottery). NCVO points to a growing dependence by charities upon grants and fees. It also appears that levels of volunteering are no better than stable.

3. Third Sector Foresight Conference, May 1997, NCVO, Henley Centre and Baring Foundation.

4. There is much disagreement as to whether British society's 'fragmentation' is being accompanied by a 'collapse' of its civil life. Bodies like the Foundation For Civil Society argue in apocalyptic terms, but probably the most careful piece of research is Professor Peter Hall, reported in Social Capital, a fragile asset (Demos Collection issue 12, 1997.) Hall challenges Robert Putnam's celebrated thesis in 'Bowling alone: America's disintegrating social capital,' and shows that the extent of voluntary association between British citizens is at worst stable and perhaps growing. He does, however, also identify the fact that this is not true of the poorest, least well-educated section of society.

5. The spread of figures here indicates disagreement in published research about definitions and scope. The lack of solid data about the third sector is a problem in its own right.

6. I am conscious of the substantial work over several years by Perri 6, Demos's Research Director and a former research director of the National Council for Voluntary Organisations. This is reflected, *inter alia*, in *Delivering Welfare* (Centre d'Iniciatives de l'Economia Social, 1994) and the journal he edits, *Non-Profit Studies*, which set itself up on a platform of 'not countenancing boosterism.' Perri 6 has argued that the charitable sector is weakened by its particularism (serving select groups of clients) and open to question in terms of its commitment to redistribution. The sector's position, he has written, 'with neither the efficiency of for-profit firms nor the fairness of government [is] sufficiently marginal to be tolerated by partisans of the two main forms.' These arguments provide an important antidote to the notion that 'voluntary is best', but their ultimately negative character distract from the important public policy task of asking not how the voluntary sector can be boosted by more tax privileges of the established sort, but how can the sector be regulated effectively, put its own house in order and receive financial privileges commensurate with its ability to deliver.

7. *Brookings Review,* Fall 1997.

8. Green D, 1993, *Reinventing Civil Society,* Istitute for Economic Affairs, London.

9. Speech in 1995; collected in *New Britain,* Fourth Estate, London, 1996.

10. Giddens A, 1998, *The Third Way: The revival of social democracy,* Polity Press, Cambridge.

11. Alun Michael's argument was summarised by him in *New Statesman,* 20 February 1998.

12. Kay J, 1998, 'Evolutionary politics', *Prospect*, July 1998.

13. The third sector created one in seven new jobs in France between 1980 and 1990 and one in eight in Germany, according to *Promoting the Role of Voluntary Organisations and Foundations in Europe*, European Commission 1997.

14. See Leadbeater C, 1997, *The Rise of the Social Entrepreneur*, Demos, London; Thake S and Zadek S, 1997, *Practical People, Noble Causes*, New Economics Foundation, London.

15. Mulgan G and Landry C, 1995, *The other invisible hand: remaking charity for the 21st century*, Demos, London.

16. The Local Government Management Board is the latest organisation to suggest a scheme of this kind, in August 1998.

17. Timmins N, 1995, *The Five Giants: A biography of the welfare state*, Harper Collins, London.

7

LEARNING BEYOND THE CLASSROOM
Tom Bentley

'I think a lot of the time at school ... they teach you knowledge but they never teach you how to learn.'

This comment, by a seventeen year old English school student, sums up the basic challenge facing education in the next century. Education has become a concern bordering on an obsession. Not only is it fundamental to individual life-chances, but more and more it is a decisive influence on our collective identity, the effectiveness of our institutions and our quality of life. Politicians proclaim their passion for it as a matter of course. Across the world, governments and interest groups are making education integral to strategies for economic development, social cohesion and risk reduction.

But the goal of a 'learning society' is still remote. Despite frenetic activity, milestones in qualifications and participation, steadily rising public and private spending, there are fundamental challenges to be met if education is really to equip people to thrive in the twenty-first century. Young people in many western societies are having more trouble perhaps than ever before in making the transition to adulthood. Persistent and unpredictable change in economy, demographics, technology, culture, values and relationships throws doubt upon the institutions we have created to deliver education.

EDUCATION, EDUCATION, EDUCATION
'Ignorance', one of Beveridge's five giant evils to be slain by the post-war welfare state, has always acted as a drag on a society's development. The general level of education during the nineteenth and twentieth centuries has been taken as a measure of progress, both economic and social, and of justice. There is a deep historical imperative for extending and developing levels of education across society, whatever the disputes about how this should be structured, managed and paid for. But other factors have re-ignited our

recognition of education's fundamental importance.

First, as Charles Leadbeater shows in chapter two of this collection, the transition to post-industrial economies means that prosperity depends on workers who are able to create, use and communicate knowledge in increasingly complex and sophisticated ways. Second, as people have become better educated, the liberal goal of learning for its own sake has been opened up to greater numbers. In the US, a large part of the 'community college' sector of higher education is effectively part of the leisure industry, although perhaps 'recreation' is a better word for it. Third, education is increasingly important to individual life-chances and mobility. Qualifications are a passport to work, social networks, cultural capital and status, intensifying the competition for high quality and high status places, and ratcheting up demand. Fourth, the relentless emphasis on innovation and productivity in organisations leads to a higher priority for learning and skills. This is true for government, where publics expect more while resisting higher taxes. It is also true for business, where the revolution in technology-driven productivity places a premium upon knowledge creation, innovation in working methods and in product development – 90 per cent of new products are no longer on the market two years after they are launched.

In short, learning, creating and applying knowledge have become a continuous imperative for individuals and organisations, giving rise to a new idea – lifelong learning. This means that people will need to return to formal education more often during their lifetime and that learning will become a more explicit goal in activities not formally designated as education, especially work. There is now more knowledge, and more demand for it, than can be contained within a public sector infrastructure. New modes of access and knowledge creation are required.

Formal knowledge has always been contained and enshrined in institutions – libraries, monasteries, factories, universities, schools. But increasingly, knowledge is accessible from outside these institutions, because of the processing and communications power of technology, and because the most valuable knowledge is carried by increasingly mobile vessels – people. The purest example of this is the Internet, which literally exists nowhere – in 'hyper space'. It is also the case that detailed knowledge now becomes redundant much faster. By the end of a four-year engineering degree, half the knowledge content of the first year will be out of date. This means that one of the apparent central purposes of education – the accumulation of knowledge – must be redefined. The true test of understanding becomes what you are able to do with the knowledge you possess, especially in contexts outside the bounds of formal educational experience.

MORE GOVERNMENT, MORE INSTITUTIONS, BUT THE WRONG RESULT

Paradoxically, the main response to these imperatives so far has been to expand the role of formally dedicated educational institutions and to extend the length of time in which people, especially the young, spend in them. In Britain, this process has lasted for the whole of the century – from the 1902 Balfour Act, which finally consolidated a national education system in England and Wales, through the Butler Act of 1944, enforcing participation in secondary education to fourteen, the Robbins Report of 1963, opening higher education to a much wider client group, the raising of the school leaving age to sixteen in the 1970s, the massive expansion of higher education during the 1980s, and the reforms of the current Labour government, which will make nursery and pre-school education available to all three and four year olds. National Targets for Education and Training and a single framework for academic and vocational qualifications all reflect this trend.

The growth of institutions has been mirrored by growth in the state's powers of intervention in education, which has been endorsed by governments of left and right.[1] The 1988 Education Act came from a government committed to 'rolling back the frontiers of the state'. But it is a trend, visible in most of the developed world, which fits with a specifically twentieth century conception of government now under extreme pressure.

Also under pressure is our view of education as a story of institutions with strong organisational hierarchies, professional status and vertical division of labour resting on defined academic or vocational subject classifications. Two traditions are reflected in this culture: the monasteries which acted as closed repositories for knowledge in the form of precious manuscripts, and the requirements of the industrial age to instil and replicate standardised knowledge, schools and colleges. The result is a curious hybrid of factory, sanctuary, prison and asylum. They aim to be safe learning environments, but also seek to contain and control their students. They seek to develop the individual strengths and capacities of learners, but are also responsible for producing standardised, Fordist outputs. They strive to produce young people who can make responsible choices, while removing many of the most important choices from them.

Despite massive change around them, these institutional forms have proved remarkably robust. However, a parallel infrastructure is also now being created, one which better fits the contours and demand patterns of contemporary society. Broadly speaking, it is an infrastructure for lifelong learning. It includes core government investment, in the UK for example in a University for Industry, a National Grid for Learning, and Individual Learning Accounts, which will allow adults to invest public, private and personal finances in their own learning choices, and it includes public–private ventures, such as the Cambridge Science Park. The precursor of this infrastructure in Britain was the Open University, a demand led, technology-based, distance learning institution which has made higher education accessible to hundreds of thousands of adult learners in ways which allow them to integrate it into their working and family lives. All of this also exists alongside an increasingly large do-it-yourself educational sector, based upon books, television, the Internet and informal methods of learning from friends and family.

These new models are demand led and individualised, employing information and communications technologies (ICTs), weak control structures and network forms of organisation. Their systems are fluid and rely on the idea that learners either know what they need or can be persuaded rather than compelled to find out. They depend on shared investment, and on utilising a wider range of resources than taxpayers' money, public building stock, professional skills and contracted parental obligation.

Much of this new infrastructure is being created by the private sector, which in Britain already spends more on training and education than the government. Examples include firm-based universities such as Rover and Unipart, where courses do not lead to formal qualifications but to increased knowledge, ability and innovation within the companies. An American model is the University of Phoenix, funded privately by fee-paying adults, whose 'library' is accessed from any on-line computer terminal, and whose 'campus' is spread across 47 different franchised sites in the western USA. The explosive growth in private provision of education, training and human resource services – groups such as Spring, which modestly describes itself as 'the future of work', or of core education providers such as the Edison Project or Nord Anglia, also show how learning systems are increasingly created and managed with private sector involvement. Multinational corporations are also showing increased interest in creating their own schools for employees in the developing world. and the World Bank is investigating the potential of private capital investment to create education infrastructures, instead of relying on development programmes run through state bureaucracies. The learning industry, like the knowledge industries, is becoming global, reflecting the continuous growth in demand for knowledge and its emerging primacy as an economic resource.

WHAT IS EDUCATION FOR?

How well can these two sets of institutions meet the learning challenges of the next century? To answer, we must ask: what is the purpose of education?

One standard answer is that it is the process by which young people are pre-pared for adulthood, recognising the prevailing risks in a society, its priori-ties and social systems.

This answer breaks down into others: if education is a process of knowl-edge acquisition, to a level which adult society deems necessary for the young to reach their station in life, it gives rise to debate about the knowl-edge content of the curriculum, the duration of compulsory education, the validity of qualifications, and the levels of achievement which different young people might be expected to reach. But it pre-supposes that we have a clear answer about what young people will need to do in the future in order to survive and thrive, which we no longer have.

Also, in suggesting that education is the transmission of norms, values and attitudes which society values, this definition of education assumes that soci-ety's dominant values and priorities are still identifiable in an era of greater plurality and diversity, which is questionable when established ways of liv-ing are fractured and eroded by change.

An answer to the question robust for any time or place is that education is the process by which the young learn to master a society's symbolic nota-tional systems and to use those systems in conjunction with the knowledge gained through intuition and direct experience, in tasks and roles which the society values. At its simplest, this means words and numbers. It also increas-ingly means the symbols and languages of information technology, along with the vocabularies, disciplines, applications and uses of all these symbol-ic systems.

One of the central and most neglected problems in testing the quality of these attempts to define educational purpose is that the value of output from schools and universities can only be judged with reference to external crite-ria – how well the knowledge and disciplines acquired through education meet the challenges which adult life and society present. Conventional qual-ifications are only proxies for the abilities they are supposed to reflect. When societies change rapidly, the currency of such qualifications is devalued. So, rather than focusing on the means – courses and qualifications – we must focus on the ends. There are three ends for which education systems should strive:

- *Autonomy:* the capacity to govern oneself, to make choices, form pur-poses, and secure the resources necessary to achieve one's goals.
- *Responsibility:* the capacity to take responsibility for oneself and one's actions, for one's children and families, and for wider society.
- *Creativity:* the capacity to think and act creatively in forming and

achieving our goals, to solve problems, to understand the structures and disciplines which shape our lives, and to apply our knowledge in ways which extend and develop it.

THE SYSTEM BREAKS DOWN

Contemporary education systems, it could be argued, provide a higher level of knowledge in symbolic languages than ever before, and a greater level of general preparation for participation in a complex adult society. But there is a serious and growing problem, as illustrated by the tension between our two sets of institutions. The old infrastructure attempts to deliver education according to a specified set of rules and processes – the standardised rhythms and routines of the school day – with a framework of knowledge and standards set by society. It represents a 'guardian syndrome' – the tendency to protect and control the young in their own, and our, best interests, by directing them through a system which is, to a large extent, pre-programmed. The new institutions, by contrast, assume that individuals, through their choices and responsibilities, will set the demand for knowledge and learning services which best serve their, and society's, interests. This is the 'trader syndrome', where people are equipped to search for new solutions to their problems, to be active, creative and entrepreneurial in combining resources to meet their needs.

This presupposes that 'educated' adults are prepared for the risks and responsibilities which they will have to meet, partly through their commitment to further learning. But the problem is that a system for educating the young which resembles a programmed machine does not necessarily prepare them to thrive in less certain, more complex environments. In short, school-based education cannot be counted on to produce young people who are equipped to become successful lifelong learners.

One reason for this is the growing disjunction between the organisational environment of the school and the rest of us. As organisations are restructured around horizontal divisions of labour, ICT capacity, and networks rather than hierarchies, the habits and routines developed in school are less useful in the real world. This also creates a series of structural barriers which help prevent schools from making better use of the knowledge resources which surround them – through relationships with parents, employers and the community, including through ICT connections.

Another is that the machine model of education, as with all machines, only performs effectively when the external conditions are relatively stable. Today, it is harder for schools to provide what young people need, because what they will need is less certain. The transition to adulthood in western societies has become more complex and drawn out. It takes longer to achieve economic independence, and the transition to employment is less straightforward, especially for those in worse-off socioeconomic groups where established industries and employment security have disappeared. Similarly, we are relearning the importance of the family to educational attainment, at a time when family life is under great pressure.

The results of these limitations are severe. They include greater emotional and psychological pressure on the young – suicide is now the second most common cause of death for eighteen to 24 year olds in the UK, and emotional and depressive disorders are increasing. Low employability among young people was recently estimated to cost the British economy £8 billion a year, and studies have shown that parents, while impressing on their children the growing importance of education to their job prospects, feel unable to give them practical guidance because they are unsure about how the world of work is really changing. Young people are poorly equipped to prepare financially for the future, with the great majority failing to save enough to give them security later in life. The growing concern about young people's capacity to form relationships, behave morally and avoid risky behaviours is a sign that the formal curriculum is not providing enough to equip them for adult life. This concern tends to focus on the disadvantaged and worse-off, but applies equally to all young people.

Added to these is the failure of educational success. Mounting evidence shows that, too often, young people who succeed in education are unable to apply what they have learned in unfamiliar contexts where the knowledge might actually be useful. This is true in all subjects and disciplines, and of adults, university graduates and schoolchildren. Producing the correct answers for examinations is not, it seems, enough to enable a learner to make use that knowledge in the wider world. The tendency to revert to basic, intuitive ideas and understandings developed in early childhood when confronted by unfamiliar problems can, all too often, coexist alongside highly developed formal and theoretical knowledge which contradicts them. In these cases, the things we learn in education institutions do not benefit us in solving questions, meeting responsibilities and making choices, although they may still help us gain access to status, income and other life-chances.

Another result is the depth of disaffection among many of the young, resulting in their leakage from the framework of institutions and the heightening of many longer-term risks such as unemployment, crime, poor health and homelessness. Hundreds of thousands of sixteen to 25 year olds in the UK are effectively marginalised, not in work, education or training, surviving through family and informal economy, unable to develop their abilities in any formally recognised way and often deeply ambivalent or hostile to education because of their experiences.

Another symptom is the growth of alternative schooling movements – some 50,000 children in the UK now learn at home, and the numbers (and proportion) are far higher in the US. Independent religious and specialist schools are also exerting growing pressure on governments for recognition and funding of their choice to bypass the core framework of institutions and to root children more firmly in their domestic social, cultural and religious context.

DE-SCHOOLING: THE IDEA WHOSE TIME HAS COME

Rapid and unsettling change reinforces the importance of education, but makes the challenge more demanding. As the rural priest in Alan Paton's great South African novel *Cry the Beloved Country* put it, having seen the wonders and evils of Johannesburg,

> 'One could go back knowing better the things that one fought against, knowing better the kind of thing that one must build. He would go back with a new and quickened interest in the school, not as a place where children learned to read and write and count only, but as a place where they must be prepared for life in any place to which they might go.'

The next great turning in education, the task of tomorrow's politicians, was first proposed by Ivan Illich almost 30 years ago.[2] It is that we must de-school society, to prepare the young to be genuinely autonomous, responsible and creative, and to continue learning throughout their adult lives. We must find ways of using the full range of resources which society can offer – not just taxpayers' money, public building stock, professional skills and contracted parental obligations, but private investment, human, cultural, physical and social capital, information and knowledge resources. This means that learning must take place, not at one remove from the adult world, but to a much greater extent actually in the contexts and communities where knowledge is employed to create value.

Achieving this change requires several shifts, all of which have foundations in the present.

Multiple intelligences

We must reframe our understanding of intelligence and ability. The twentieth century view of intelligence as a single, scientifically measurable entity, both fixed and inherited, has effectively been undermined by research and practice which shows intelligence to be far broader and more diverse. Howard Gardner's theory of multiple intelligences, setting out eight different clusters, including logical-mathematical, interpersonal, musical and spatial intelligence, provides a way of viewing human capacity which offers a wider range of entry points to genuine understanding.[3] Everybody has a profile of these eight, determined partly by our genes and neural networks, but they are found in different combinations and degrees, influencing the ways in which we best develop and demonstrate understanding. Most education is currently organised around two of these intelligences – logical-mathematical and linguistic – but education for all must be able to nurture and employ the full range in order to reach its full potential.

Demonstrating understanding

We must develop the methods and instruments by which we assess understanding, to test its depth and range beyond merely producing the right responses under controlled conditions. Understanding is developed through a combination of thought and practice, and is only genuinely demonstrated in contexts where the knowledge concerned is of real value. This emerging 'performance' view of understanding is related to the practice of 'competence-based assessment', but requires more rigour and depth.[4] It implies that educational achievements should be assessed not just by academics, teachers and universities, but by a far wider range of experts from the field connected with a specific area of learning. It also implies that educational outcomes should be understood in broader terms: readiness for the fundamental responsibilities of adult life, work, parenting, citizenship and the capacity to take responsibility oneself, rather than the qualifications which currently act as proxies for readiness.

Valued roles

To understand the uses and value of the knowledge which they gain in education, young learners must be given greater exposure to the roles and responsibilities of adult life. In order to answer the question on so many young lips – what's the point? – and to develop the capacity to develop and apply knowledge, education must provide greater experience of the ways in which formal knowledge are used in society. This means learning in workplaces, families, communities and elsewhere. It means young people learning from each other and having responsibility for passing on their knowledge and accumulated experience. Projects such as Children's Express, the young people's journalism project which involves its members in investigating and writing, publishing and broadcasting stories about issues affecting young people, or Changemakers, which supports teams of school pupils to conceive, plan and execute community projects aimed at meeting a need they have identified, are among the many exemplars in this field. This kind of educational experience gives young people real responsibility and demonstrates how knowledge and skills are employed and applied in adult society, while challenging them to integrate their formal knowledge with their goals, expectations and understanding of the world outside school.

Learning relationships

If learning and knowledge are less contained within institutions, we must rediscover the importance of relationships as tools for developing under-standing and ability. Learning relationships frame the acquisition of knowl-edge and the development of understanding, and locate them in the values and purposes of individuals, communities and society. The most important for education are parenting, teaching, mentoring and apprenticeship. Creating, strengthening and sustaining these relationships will become increasingly important for education systems, and learning relationships will become recognised as the connections through which knowledge, judge-ment and understanding are developed. They also offer a better way of developing inter-personal understanding and relationship skills. The fact that young people are most likely to describe the attributes of a good teacher in terms of the quality of their working relationship with students is no acci-dent. But learning relationships will have to extend far beyond schools and school timetables. The recent growth of mentoring programmes in the UK and US is another foundation of this change.

Schools as neighbourhood learning centres

Schools and colleges, to play their part in this learning revolution, must be opened up to become community assets. This means acting as hubs for a wide range of activities, from local democracy to adult learning, community celebrations to citizens' advice. Schools must become networked, not just with ICTs, but with the overlapping, mutual networks of community and economic life. Education plays such a powerful part in individual and fami-ly lives that learning institutions have the potential to become a focus for community life which few institutions, including religious ones, now pos-sess. To do this they must be open for longer, provide a wider range of infor-mation and opportunity, and be able to draw in the knowledge and com-mitment which surround them to help achieve their core purposes. They will do this not by trying to provide all services themselves, but by acting as bro-kers for a far wider range of opportunities and resources.

Contributing to the knowledge economy

We should build on the growing and direct contribution of education institutions to a knowledge economy, to maximise the resources and opportunities for learning. A system of work experience which actually combined sustained work placements and responsibilities with school or college based
courses, such as that developed in Australia, would give far greater insight
into the relationship between education and work than the current British
system of two-week work experience placements. In 1997, a 17 year-old
beat several high-profile companies to win a Website of the Year award for
a site which he had designed in his bedroom as a birthday present for his
younger sister. In 1996, a Local Education Authority entered a legal dispute
with a software company over the intellectual property rights for a games
programme written by a student on a school computer and subsequently
sold to the company for development. Rather than seeing economic responsibility and opportunity as a hazard for young people, we should be using
it – with appropriate safeguards – as an opportunity to develop their understanding, generate resources and draw in a wider range of people and institutions to education.

The science and art of thoughtfulness

Thinking skills, and the benefits that they yield, have been systematically
neglected by western education systems for too long. There is now enough
rigorous evidence from research and practice to show that paying more and
better attention to the structures and disciplines of thinking can produce dramatic improvements in formal educational attainment. CASE (Cognitive
Acceleration in Science Education) is one example from the UK, but there
are many more. But thinking not only improves our ability to pass exams, it
also increases our capacity to act intelligently in all the realms of life. That
is why it is an art as well as a science, and why paying better attention to
'meta-cognitive' development is key to re-establishing the connections
between education and the challenges of adult life.[5] This fact requires us to
move towards more individualised curricula which allow learners to probe
and uncover the deep structure of the subjects and disciplines they study.
Thinking in these ways also allows education to make clearer the purposes
and underlying motivations which fuel the desire to learn. Genuine creativity requires rigour, depth and an understanding of the underlying structures
of problems, rather than more superficial forms of expression.
Thoughtfulness is an indispensable precondition.

WHAT TOMORROW'S POLITICIANS SHOULD DO

Rather than a single public education infrastructure, governments should concentrate on establishing the standards, outcomes and underlying bases needed to support learning opportunities. The challenge is to create complex systems of learning which can combine formal and informal resources around the needs and abilities of individual learners.

This challenge is framed by the relationship between three factors: the identities of learners, the systems of provision through which they learn, and the outcomes which the interaction between these two produce. A requirement that education should continue to sixteen or beyond does not mean that it must take place only in school. A public knowledge infrastructure, accessible through schools, homes, libraries, firms, universities, community centres and voluntary organisations, should underpin the range of teaching and learning services offered by increasingly diverse providers. Capital investment in ICTs should include connecting schools and colleges with homes, and should be accompanied by equal investment in technology skills. The corporate tax regime should reflect the level of investment by companies in learning resources for employees, their families and surrounding communities. Local and regional agencies should also make use of 'knowledge planning gain', working to ensure that new investment and development creates benefits for the learning resources available in a given area.

Funding should be increasingly individualised, with weightings for specific adversities or special needs. This does not mean a crude market in education vouchers, but a funding system which allows individual learners to access more flexible packages of learning from a range of providers. Curriculum delivery should also be individualised, emphasising less of the standardised consistency of institutions and examination boards, and more the rigorous coherence of disciplined individual learning. Guidance and advisory services, focusing on the expectations of learners and their parents, and the ways in which they articulate and develop their goals, should be strengthened. A portfolio of continuous assessment and recording of achievement, utilising increasingly rich data sources, should extend from the earliest years of a learning career into adulthood. Assessment information should increasingly include the perspectives and judgements of learners, both of their own performance and the quality of their educational experience. Mentoring programmes should be expanded, giving young people, especially disadvantaged ones, access to role models and networks which education does not currently provide. The focus on innovation and the spread of good ideas and best practice should be strengthened.

A fourth tier of educational employment, in community learning, should be created through the spread of learning networks outward from existing institutions. Greater attention should be paid to the interfaces between education and other activities, by appointing school–community brokers, creating teaching posts which span education and industry, and encouraging social and civic entrepreneurs to generate new solutions and systems at community level. The Cooperative Education Movement in Canada, which creates employment opportunities for students to apply the knowledge gained in their degree courses, was invented by Waterloo University. Waterloo is now ranked as the one of the most consistent suppliers of high quality graduates to the information and creative industries in North America. Voluntary effort, through mentoring, masterclasses and community campaigns for literacy and other learning goals, should be stimulated and nurtured. Per capita funding should, as in Denmark and the Netherlands, be made available to parents and other groups wishing to establish schools, as long as they can demonstrate their ability to achieve the outcomes and quality standards which governments must continue to set and monitor.

As children gain in understanding and age, they should take increasing responsibility for their own learning. The infrastructure for learning out of school hours, through museums, libraries, sports clubs, supermarkets and study centres, should be expanded. From birth to sixteen, children currently spend only 15 per cent of their waking time at school. Schools and colleges should be open from early morning to late at night, offering multi-purpose facilities for cradle-to-grave learning. Funding should be geared towards the early years, when educational support makes most difference. Integrated records of learning careers, based on individual learner numbers rather than fragmented institutional records, and with appropriate safeguards for privacy, should be developed. Employment policy should recognise the demands of parenting and be structured to support family learning. Transport policy should create new, safe ways for children and young people to travel safely between learning sites. Attainment should be assessed and measured as much through performance, application and problem-solving as through the repetition of standardised tasks under controlled conditions.

WELCOME TO THE LEARNING SOCIETY

At the end of the twentieth century, we have lost many of the great totalising narratives of the industrial age. Communism has collapsed, and faith in the power of markets has been tempered by the recognition that they do not provide the answer to everything. Markets are embedded in social norms, beliefs and cultures, and depend on them for their effectiveness as systems of exchange. While religion still plays a strong part in our spiritual lives, in western societies it lacks the ability to control and fixate that it possessed.

There is, however, one overarching story which has proved more enduring. It is a story of generalised 'progress', driven by economic, technological and scientific development, realised through rising living standards, upward mobility and self-improvement. Because it allows us to focus mainly on our own lives and the difference we can make to them, it emphasises personal freedom, the space within which we can do as we choose. Learning and education play a powerful role in this compelling story.

But there is always a choice. The narratives that have lost their grip seem to be ones that have put too much faith in one source of knowledge. Whether it is an account of history, like Marxism, of the meaning and purpose of life, like Christianity, or the power of an organisational framework, like the market, they have assumed that they can provide a definitive, closed account of what matters and what that means for our lives. The narrative of progress that we are left with, on the other hand, seems only to give us stories that make sense for individuals and specific social groups, driven by underlying forces of change. The ways in which these individual stories combine do not produce a coherent, compelling vision of how society as a whole might develop. As a result, it cannot give any meaningful guidance about how we resolve the tensions and collisions that arise from our interdependence: the clash between different forms of social identity, between generations, between economic dynamism and environmental sustainability, between wealth creation and social inclusion.

There is, however, another view of progress, which recognises the uniqueness of each of us and our place in the story, but also recognises the complexity of the systems that govern us and our development. Such a view means that we can believe in progress, without assuming that we know everything needed to achieve it. We can hope that society can learn to do better, just as we hope this for ourselves and our children. In short, we can believe in a learning society.

Education is no longer the one-way transmission of information and knowledge, but the patterns of interaction that allow us to acquire new information, develop disciplines which lead to greater understanding, and discover shared meaning through mutual comprehension.

For adults, this is perhaps the most difficult and challenging dimension of the learning society. Continuous learning involves forgetting as well as remembering. To solve new problems, we must be able to cast aside assumptions and models that no longer serve us well. All of us have a deeply ingrained set of assumptions about what education is, some positive, many negative, because it is an experience that all of us have been through. But if we want our learning to reflect current reality, we must be able to question these assumptions and to understand what it is really like to be a young person growing up now. This involves a fundamental shift of power between older and younger generations. It means recognising that we do not have all the answers, and that we can learn from the young as well as teaching them. It means taking them seriously, putting time, effort and care into our dealings with them, providing secure, fertile social environments in which they can learn their way around, and becoming actively involved in their learning.

If we do make the shift, we will be able to measure our learning not by the amount of money we spend on it, or by the number of certificates we have, but by our success in solving real problems, the time and care that we put into our own learning, our health and well-being, and the extent of our mutual understanding and shared achievement. Then, and only then, will we be on the road to the learning society.

Tom Bentley's book, *Learning Beyond the Classroom: Education for a changing world*, is published by Routledge.

NOTES

1. Green A, 1990, *Education and State Formation: The rise of education systems in England, France and the USA*, Macmillan, London.

2. Illich I, 1973, *De-Schooling Society*, Penguin, Harmondsworth.

3. Gardner H, 1983, *Frames of Mind: The theory of multiple intelligences*, Basic Books, New York.

4. Wiske MS, 1998, *Teaching for Understanding: Linking research with practice*, Jossey Bass, San Fransisco.

5. Perkins, D, 1995, *Outsmarting IQ: The emerging science of learnable intelligence*, Free Press, New York

8

ECOPOLIS: TOMORROW'S POLITICS OF THE ENVIRONMENT

Ian Christie

A radical 'Third Way' has already been discovered. Remarkably, much of the planet has grudgingly signed up to follow it, at least in theory. It is outlined in the grey prose of Agenda 21, the key declaration on environmentally sustainable development from the Earth Summit of 1992 at Rio. The problem is that although we have found one of the keys to tomorrow's politics, we are reluctant to use it, or to believe the evidence that it will work. 'The environment' may be the great discovery of the past generation – front page news, the source of truly pioneering ideas, innovations and international agreements – but it is not yet integrated into mainstream economic life and political argument. This essay explores how emerging approaches to environmentalism can shape tomorrow's politics.

The core argument is that there is a path of 'eco-modernisation' that will enable us to meet the challenge which has defeated both the new right and the old social democratic left: full employment with environmental sustainability. There cannot be a worthwhile Third Way if it fails to take both these goals seriously, but it will not be easy for the political representatives of 'Mondeo Man'. Tomorrow's politicians must act upon the overwhelming evidence that ecologically sustainable development is not only *needed* for survival but is *desirable* as a force for better quality of life. The key claims made here are these:

- Environmentalism has achieved a huge shift in opinion and policy in much of the developed world; but it has under-achieved politically.
- Greens and proponents of political modernisation need each other. Environmentalism can only break through by linking itself to a realistic vision of progress; but a new politics seeking to combine market dynamism with community and decency, and to revive trust and participation in the democratic process, needs the civic energy and ethical spirit of environmentalism.

- 'Eco-modernisation' brings these agendas together to: promote an advanced service economy and fight unemployment; to make government and public services work better; and to reinvigorate democracy and community life, especially at local level.

THE REAL THIRD WAY – THE PROGRESS OF ENVIRONMENTALISM

In the 1990s the end of ideology has been announced, but the analysis is wrong. Environmentalism offers the missing ideological framework, based upon its already considerable achievements.[1] Ministries of the environment exist throughout the world. In advanced countries, the worst pollution of air and rivers has been cleaned up and global action has begun: the Montreal Protocol on ozone-depleting chemicals; the Rio Summit of 1992, with its Agenda 21 programme of action for the next century; and the Kyoto Summit of 1997, which – however disappointing in the targets set for 'greenhouse gas' reduction – established a global regime for coordinated action to move away from energy-intensive development based on fossil fuels. This is to a large extent the work of non-governmental organisations (NGOs) which have built up campaigning resources and popular trust on a scale which often exceeds that of mainstream political parties.

The core principle around which this achievement has been constructed is that of 'sustainable development',[2] defined in the 1987 Brundtland Report as: 'development which meets the needs of the present without compromising the ability of future generations to meet their own needs'. This idea is based on a global diagnosis:

- There will be 8 billion people on the earth by 2025. If we are to have current western levels of per capita income for the developing countries in the next half-century, the OECD world will need a gigantic improvement in technological efficiency just to hold resource consumption and emissions at current levels.
- Industrial economies have treated the natural world as an infinite bank of resources and as an infinite dump for wastes. But many resources are not renewable, and there are limits to the 'absorption capacity' of ecosystems.
- In particular, the rise in CO_2 and other greenhouse gases from fossil fuel use is leading to global warming, likely to disrupt climate in damaging and possibly disastrous ways.
- Diffusion of toxic chemicals, and of chemicals or man-made organisms whose environmental impact is largely unknown, threatens biodiversity and poses long-term public health risks.
- Growth and all the goods which flow from it depend on 'critical natural

capital' – the healthy operation of natural 'services' in the atmosphere, oceans and other systems. We can find substitutes for many non-renewable resources but there are key common goods which cannot be replaced. The environmental costs of growth have not been integrated into measures of growth or the prices of goods and services.

It is true that some details are disputed, but the diagnosis is widely accepted. Politics, therefore, cannot ignore a set of major socioeconomic consequences:

- The growing population of the developing world, and especially the fifth of humanity living in absolute poverty, has an unanswerable moral claim to improve its living standards. If it does so on the western model, many ecosystems would be strained to the point of collapse. Developing countries need help to modernise their economies on sustainable lines.
- The industrialised world is largely responsible for the worst threats, especially global warming. Thus it should bear most of the costs of finding solutions.
- Acceptance of limits to 'business as usual' raises issues of equity across generations, between the rich and low-income worlds, and between rich and poor in the developed world. We need new ways of distributing 'fair shares' of consumption: innovations such as CO_2 futures trading, ways to allocate shares in 'environmental space' – levels of consumption of energy and materials by households, organisations and countries.[3]
- This points to the inevitability of judgement being made about consumption choices, and to the need for policies and institutions based on principles of mutual rights and responsibilities to protect the 'commons' from damage by cumulative individual choices.
- This in turn implies mechanisms for achieving consent in limiting unsustainable consumption and production, and for high trust in government and business. We need new forms of partnership and networking between sectors and levels of government.
- Transition to sustainable development demands new information about how the economy affects the environment and new ways of valuing economic activity.

Here is the outline of a politics radically different from the neoliberal economic consensus, which also challenges a social democracy that sees progress substantially in terms of widening individuals' access to private goods. The sustainability agenda 're-legitimises' debates and policies neglected in the years of market liberalisation. In this it parallels the rediscovery by left and right alike of social capital and trust as essential for long-term economic progress. Prosperity depends not only on productivity but also on the quality of the public commons – ecological and social – which make private choices and market operations possible.

The sustainability imperative also calls for new thinking about the state. Government cannot plan for and deliver sustainable development on its own; neither can it leave everything to voluntarism and the market. It is a broker of partnerships, a builder of frameworks for action by business and other groups, and a negotiator at international level. It should cultivate a sense of ownership, trust and agency among citizens if they are to be motivated to change; and it needs to promote as much diversity as possible in experimentation for sustainable solutions. Sustainability demands smart subsidiarity – we need not only national and local action, but also greater accountability and integration of policy at international level about globalisation and sustainability.

FROM HERE TO SUSTAINABILITY? THE HARD POLITICS OF THE ENVIRONMENT
Why is it that, despite environmentalism's achievements, activism has hit a plateau and its political impact been subdued?

Firstly, green NGOs have developed a reputation as scaremongers. We still know too little about the ecological limits to 'business as usual' to predict how much of a given activity will push an ecosystem over the edge. As new information emerges and risk assessments are revised, excessive claims damage credibility and confuse the public – although it has to be said that citizens' trust in NGO information is far greater than it is in government and business claims about the environment. Moreover, there is a science-fiction aura around many eco-risks: global warming, while almost certainly real and serious, seems too huge and exotic an issue to grip politicians, media and citizens; and its science is still sufficiently uncertain to give ammunition to the 'contrarians' who argue that we do not have a problem.

Secondly, environmentalists have failed sufficiently to acknowledge the extent to which traditional growth has felt like real progress for so many people, and to which environmental gains have been made, largely as a result of their own success. The anti-industrial, nostalgic strain in 'deep Green' ideology has little political purchase in North or South; greenery needs to be about the reform and positive use of science and technology to civilise industrialism.

Thirdly, green concerns have a limited social base. Environmentalism is middle-class, professional and white for the most part, and its public image is largely about conservation, countryside and wildlife. Messages about how environmentalism could improve life chances have not been well communicated to the poor, to ethnic minority citizens, to city-dwellers or to other groups concerned with social exclusion.

At the same time, business (and Conservative politicians) have often seen environmentalism as a threat to its values, just as many on the left suspected it as a threat to jobs, higher living standards and opportunities for the poor. Despite the rhetorical acceptance of sustainability on all sides, these attitudes persist. Greens, like others in search of the Third Way, need a vision that can convince hesitant mainstream politicians, one which combines competitiveness with social cohesion and hope about jobs and quality of life.

But as Tom Burke has argued, we now face the 'hard politics' of the environment.[4] Much environmental action has been about cleaning up 'point' sources of pollution and dealing with specific threats to habitats. No one claims that these tasks are over, especially in the developing world. But in the west the policies are largely in place. But this is not so for the big problems identified at Rio – CO_2 emissions, loss of biodiversity and over-consumption of critical resources.

The most serious damage now comes from 'diffuse' sources – millions of vehicle exhausts, millions of consumer choices demanding energy from fossil fuels, the accumulation of toxic chemicals in food chains, over-fishing of seas, or decline of overall biodiversity in habitats. These focus attention on the undesirable consequences of entire productive systems and on the need for restructuring whole sectors of energy-intensive industry, and shifting mass patterns of consumption.

As a result, says Burke, 'the buck stops everywhere'. This means that there are many more potential losers than in previous phases of eco-politics. It points to the need to engage actors at every political level and runs up against most citizens' lack of a sense of 'ownership' – of either the problems or the capacity to help solve them. This helps explain the sense of political stasis.

Green 'micro-politics' – influencing business and local government, and lobbying national and international agencies – is nonetheless making progress, for example in persuading corporations to account for and improve their environmental and social impacts.[5] Naming and shaming by NGOs – as experienced by Shell and Nike – goes hand in hand with new collaborations between campaigners and multinationals in implementing codes for ethical trading and sustainable sourcing in forestry and fishing. The gradual acceptance by firms such as Shell and BP of demands for greater transparency, and for constructive action on global warming, sends a powerful signal to others.

Genuine progress has also been made in the greening of local government and tapping the energies of local communities. The action plan Local Agenda 21 (LA21) has been a catalyst for innovation, promoting new forms of consultation with citizens, partnerships for more sustainable economic regeneration and work on new indicators of quality of life.[6] At its best, LA21 has demonstrated the potential of a new civic environmentalism to revive engagement in planning and local democracy, which have both lost popular trust and interest.

Still more important, green campaigns, almost alone in an age of disenchantment about politics, can bring people on to the streets and generate passionate debate and action, drawing attention as no mainstream political force has done to the problems of disconnection in modern societies:

- the detachment of business and investors from the ultimate environmental and social impacts of their activities
- the physical and informational distance between consumers and the sources of their purchases – most obvious in the case of food – and their detachment from the ethical and environmental implications of production
- the disconnection between the virtual markets of global finance and the material basis and social ends of economies.

Environmentalism is thus a force for new thinking about the means of reconnection of citizens with decision-making in government and business, and about the remoralisation of economic choices.[7] The articulation of unease and demand for debate about the risks posed by genetically modified organisms is the latest example, but others abound. We now have a nascent environmental and ethical investment industry and a growing organic farming and distribution sector. Both have stimulated new thinking about mutualism and have begun to influence policy-makers and business. NGOs have been instrumental in exposing the failure of international agencies to manage globalisation in ways compatible with sustainability. It is because of NGOs such as World Wide Fund for Nature working with business, that we have voluntary codes of 'stewardship' for sustainable fishing and forestry. They and their corporate partners are important social and economic innovators, unaided by the state. If governments and global agencies showed a fraction of this innovative capacity, or had the will to promote it more strongly, we would already be travelling along a sustainable Third Way in politics.

Tom Burke suggests that this micro-political incrementalism is probably the best we can hope for and that we need to rely mainly on NGOs and business to collaborate in the 'sustainability transition' of the next half-century. This is too pessimistic. Firstly, change is unlikely to be fast enough to prevent global environmental health worsening. Secondly, sustainability demands coordinated action at all levels and between sectors. Only governments can set up the national and global framework within which this can happen, and give a lead which can truly force the pace.

Given enough pressure, government can bite the bullet. For example, despite the overwhelming trend towards increased car use, strong lobbying and growing evidence of the costs of congestion have led to a slow revolution in transport policy in the UK. Like everything else to do with Britain's shambolic public transport system, the Government's planned 'integrated transport strategy' is likely to be held up by lack of political willpower, but its themes reflects a huge concession to environmental arguments, calling for a shift from road to public transport, walking and cycling, and to reducing the need for travel. In the teeth of a culture in which a majority of young adults say they value a driving licence more highly than the right to vote[8] this is a radical move, and an acceptance of the need for tough choices about charging for road use which may create many 'losers'. Similar shifts in attitude may be in prospect over two emotive issues – genetically modified organisms and food, and the increasingly bitter arguments over where to build new homes. In both cases, Government could seize the opportunity to open up national debate on sustainability, the implications of our lifestyle choices and the kind of environment and other public goods we wish to have.

But overall, progress is blocked at the level of the 'macro-politics' of the environment: the lack of will among national governments to drive the process of mainstreaming sustainable development and living up to the demands of Rio, Kyoto and Agenda 21. The greening of business is held back by the lack of carrot-and-stick incentives to adopt cleaner production systems, to save energy in a world of cheap fuel and to report on environmental impacts. Environmental and social/ethical auditing and reporting are hampered by a lack of consistent standards. The greening of local communities is limited by constrained financial resources and powers in local government.

Gestures of leadership have been made – as with Britain and Germany's declared intent to reduce greenhouse gas emissions by 2010 by well above the dismal 8 per cent cut on 1990 levels agreed at Kyoto for the EU as a whole. But so far governments and mainstream parties have reacted to environmentalism in general and the challenge of Rio and Kyoto in particular rather than drive their initiatives forward with confidence.

Of course, if we reach a point of eco-emergency governments will have no choice in the matter; and if we reach such a pass then the economic and social fabric will be at risk too. But there are better reasons for change than that. The environmental agenda can help achieve non-environmental goals at the heart of politics: reconnecting a healthy economy with low unemployment; rebuilding a high level of trust and participation in local democracy; and creating a modernised government system which makes the most of public money to achieve outcomes that people want.

MOVING SUSTAINABILITY TO CENTRE STAGE: THE PROMISE OF ECO-MODERNISATION

In the face of the challenge of 'hard politics', environmentalists have forged pragmatic alliances with business and governments for realistic, incremental change, and built links with social justice organisations.[9] Sustainability is now typically defined by NGOs, firms and governments in terms of three dimensions, which must be reconciled and kept in balance – environmental, economic and social.

This 'triple bottom line' approach, popularised by environmentalists such as John Elkington and reflected in the UK government's consultation paper on a sustainable development strategy,[10] risks reducing the concept to an 'apple pie' aspiration. But the need to take account of economic and social realities and trade-offs has prompted new thinking about strategies for a transition to sustainability. Greens know that they must advance non-environmental arguments for embracing environmentalism. The emerging story is that of ecological modernisation. This says that there are more 'sacrifices' involved in sticking to 'business as usual' than in pursuing sustainability. Decoupling economic development from growth in energy consumption and pollution can help recouple it to job creation and quality of life, as well as meeting CO_2 reduction targets.

Environmentalists, leading businesses and thoughtful economists agree it is possible to create a thriving economy while reducing pollution, waste and energy consumption.[11] This can be done by applying the disciplines of cleaner production systems – approaches to product and process design and manufacture which minimise waste, reduce energy inputs and improve efficiency of production though preventive industrial design and management. The result is reduced material and energy intensity and less pollution per unit of output.

There is a mass of theoretical analysis, case study evidence and technological development which supports this:[12] according to some estimates, we have the means already to improve our eco-efficiency by at least a factor of four. A mountain of reports tells us that huge gains in energy efficiency and savings could be made that would produce rapid paybacks, and that large numbers of jobs can be created in environmental sectors – insulation, recycling, renewable energy, forestry.

So an 'eco-capitalism' could emerge, based on continuing innovation and efficiency gains. But if so much is possible and it brings such benefits, why is it not happening spontaneously through market forces? The argument of eco-modernisers is that there is no such thing as 'the' market – a system that must be taken as a given. What we have in reality is a network of interacting markets and policy frameworks whose rules can and should be changed.

Most obviously, we need to reconnect taxation to penalise things we wish to discourage, such as pollution, not things we value, such as jobs. There is a powerful case for ecological tax reform, which will progressively raise the cost of energy and non-renewable resources, and which will offset these costs through cuts in other taxes, such as those on labour. Many studies suggest strongly that such measures, combined with policies for earmarking of eco-tax revenues for investment in energy saving, recycling, public transport, the repopulation of public services such as park-keeping, can create a 'double dividend' of reduced pollution and energy use and greatly increased employment – Tindale and Holtham suggest well over 500,000 new jobs by 2005 could be created by green tax reform packages.[13]

Another source of unsustainability is the perversity of subsidies and regulatory incentives. Norman Myers has estimated that global subsidy for unsustainable practices in agriculture, transport and energy is over $1 trillion per year, and many analysts have pointed to the lack of integration between the economic regulation of energy, focused on liberalisation and reduced costs to consumers, and environmental needs.[14] Incredibly, given Britain's Kyoto commitments, 'green' electricity from renewable sources in the new competitive market for supply is more expensive than CO_2-intensive power, and renewable energy subsidies are far lower than tax breaks for oil exploration. The new Fabian Society Commission on Taxation and the Government's review of utility regulation should be complemented by a national review of subsidy and environmental regulation across all sectors, to identify perverse incentives and set out a long-term programme of reallocating subsidy and redesigning regulations to reward activities which contribute to CO_2 reduction, generate jobs and improve quality of life.

The regulatory process also has many shortcomings. Eco-regulation is often seen as a costly top-down command-and-control mechanism which inhibits innovation and enterprise. But regulation need not impose rigid techniques and standards. It should be about using a diverse range of instruments to reward progress towards sustainability targets and to encourage change throughout whole productive systems. Regulation should embrace new eco-reporting requirements and public purchasing codes, eco-taxes and tools such as 'covenants' – voluntary agreements between government and industrial sectors and other groups for meeting long-range goals for emission cuts, backed up with the prospect of more direct intervention if targets are not met. This allows firms to experiment and innovate in ways that minimise costs, rather than taking a one-size-fits-all approach. Other developments in this area go with the grain of Charles Leadbeater's analysis in chapter two of 'dematerialisation' – trends towards a knowledge-intensive service economy. Many utilities and manufacturers are beginning to see themselves as service providers – of heating and lighting, say, rather than producers of electricity. Eco-modernisation would promote regulatory mechanisms to base utilities' profit and reward systems on service measures and sustainability targets. We can and should reward utilities for delivering services with less resource consumption instead of encouraging them to shift ever more units of output.

Progress with eco-modernisation thus requires seveal key ingredients from governments:

- willingness to push for tough greenhouse gas reductions in the face of resistance from energy-intensive interests, offering clear targets for achieving change, with the prospect of eco-taxes on fossil fuels as a stick to encourage action
- willingness to take a lead even in the absence of coordinated action by other countries: providing reasonably long lead times and imaginative incentives are devised, it is highly unlikely that businesses will relocate even in the face of unilateral eco-tax reform
- willingness to use ecological tax reform to cut energy consumption and to use revenues for job creation, support for low-income groups and green infrastructure investment
- new mechanisms to build concensus and trust in relation to eco-modernisation; greening the economy is bound up with modernising democracy and government (this crucial point is elaborated below).

TOWARDS THE ECOPOLIS: SUSTAINABILITY AND GOVERNANCE
Achieving the consensus and trust needed for eco-modernisation is vital. Much recent research reveals the profound sense of lack of control, trust and agency felt by many citizens in the face of environmental problems, declining quality of life and remote decisions by government and business.[15] Citizens need messages and evidence that what they do for the environment

counts, and that their anxieties can gain a hearing. Strategies to build up trust and agency need to be built on two broad areas of political reform: developing more holistic policy-making at all levels of government, and revitalising local democracy and planning.

Holistic government, whose virtues are set out more fully in chapter five by Perri 6, is about government by outcome-oriented measurement rather than inputs, and an emphasis on changing cultures of behaviour using 'soft' policy tools. This approach is ideal for sustainability strategies.

A holistic approach to eco-modernisation would embed consideration of the environment into all areas of policy. The creation of a Sustainable Development Unit in the Department of the Environment, Transport and the Regions is a step forward; still better would be to locate this operation in the Cabinet Office, with senior staff from the Treasury and other key economic departments, and for it to be chaired jointly by the prime minister and chancellor. Strong measures are needed to ensure that every department and agency reports on its performance against sustainability targets.

A holistic government would seek to change cultures: by integrating sustainability education in school, engineering and business education curricula; by offering business tax incentives to encourage cleaner production systems, programmes of investment in local communities and environmental/ethical reporting; and by promoting local multi-sector partnerships in support of Local Agenda 21 and in energy saving.[16] It would also seek a coherent national and EU system for eco-labelling of goods. GDP measures need to reflect environmental and social quality of life – as in the Index of Sustainable Economic Welfare (ISEW) proposed by New Economics Foundation and others,[17] and in the many local sustainability indicator sets developed through LA21.

In pursuit of this culture-changing agenda, holistic government would set itself up as an 'early adopter' of sustainability policies. It would be serious about cutting energy consumption in the public sector, placing a duty of pursuit of sustainable development targets on regulators, utilities, regional authorities and local government. It would use the purchasing power of the public sector to force the pace of market development.

Finally, holistic thinking needs to be promoted urgently at international and local levels to ensure that global accords on sustainability work, and that agreements on trade, debt, support for vulnerable economies and investment reinforce rather than undermine environmental and social strategies. Leadership and exemplary conduct by Britain and partners such as Germany are crucial in persuading other states and agencies to take sustainability seriously. The climate change regime shakily set up at Kyoto urgently needs support from other agencies in the global tier of governance – the World Trade Organisation, IMF, World Bank and OECD. Sustainability opens up a vista of new initiatives on 'transnational democracy' and a new culture for international agencies. The short-term priority is to embed holistic policy disciplines in the dis-integrated work of the IMF, WTO, G8 and other international agencies. In the longer term, imaginative experiments could be tried to propel the agenda – such as setting up a House of the Global Commons as a second chamber of the UN, with representation of all the major international agencies, business associations and NGOs, to debate and monitor the progress of the Kyoto and Rio accords.

At the local level, the revitalisation of democracy is vital. Environmentalism needs strong local government: sustainability demands a mass of local experiments, as there is no blueprint available for top-down implementation. But local democracy needs environmentalism: it is a key source of civic energy and public motivation. It is at the local level that 'the environment' becomes a real issue for most citizens: traffic jams, loss of green space, decaying estates, litter, pollution. The modernisation of local democracy, holistic government and the pursuit of local sustainability are aspects of the same agenda .

All of these things come together in the idea of planning – a concept crying out for reinvention and rehabilitation. For most citizens, 'planning' is shorthand for the creation of ugly and unsafe environments, the imposition by faceless authorities of unwanted roads, buildings and housing, or failures by local government to provide the amenities and services people want. There is no dodging a revival of planning as a systematic process of negotiation about trade-offs between private and public goods, and best options for reducing trade-offs between the economic, ecological and social dimensions of development. It is essential for implementing sustainable development and gaining trust and participation in local democracy.

Collaborative planning also sets localism in a much larger framework, with global agencies and national government, as in the Dutch National Environmental Policy Plan (NEPP). This relies not only on green taxation and traditional regulation, but draws heavily on 'soft' regulatory approaches such as covenants, public information campaigns and new forms of community consultation, along with schemes for joint implementation of CO_2 reduction targets with other countries.

Planning for sustainability is not about imposition of top-down blueprints or command-and-control direction of local economies: it is about devising flexible frameworks for meeting agreed goals, within which as much diversity and 'richness for purpose' among initiatives is encouraged. We need as much experimentation as possible with tools for social learning, consultation and participation by citizens in planning and arguing about local priorities and trade-offs. Many have been piloted via LA21: they include citizens' juries, 'visioning' conferences and new neighbourhood councils.

Innovation in planning will not count for much without real devolution of power and finance to localities. Britain leads the world in good ideas about Local Agenda 21 but leaves local communities with few resources to act on them, and the absence of a duty to implement LA21 marginalises it politically. We need to give localities real capacity to implement changes, which means more money and scope to improve local services, and clear linkages between new taxes and improved public goods. This means reforms such as earmarking of new local eco-taxes to investment in local jobs and infra-structures – for which the ground has been laid in the UK with the hypothecated landfill tax and proposed taxes on car use in towns.

CONCLUSION

Today's politics balks at the tough challenges of the next environmental agenda. Tackling 'diffuse' ecological problems implies policies which affect not only sectoral interests but millions of consumers too. Politicians talk a good game about sustainability, but few have shown the vision and courage to walk the talk. They seem to prefer to wait for change to be forced upon them by eco-emergencies. This is a wasted opportunity on an epic scale. A wealth of evidence tells us that more radical greening of the economy can help deliver more jobs, better quality of life and competitiveness.

'Eco-modernisation' is about a radical, phased restructuring process for industry and for the tax system. It also depends on modernisation of government and holistic policy-making at all levels. It connects environmental goals with progress to sustainable development for a better life. This does not mean that every policy is a 'win-win' option; it does mean that we have the resources to compensate losers in the transition and offer gains to many other social groups. It demands courage to persuade people and businesses to accept tough trade-offs in the short term between environment and economic development. But the benefits will not simply be environmental: they include a reconnection of citizens with government, and of the economy with job creation. A government is in power which has the majority and the declared will to establish sustainable development as a key element of tomorrow's politics. If not now, when?

Notes

1. M. Jacobs, 1997, *Greening the Millennium: the new politics of the environment*, Blackwell/Political Quarterly, Oxford.

2. M. Jacobs, 1991, *The Green Economy*, Pluto Press, London; McLaren D, Bullock S and Yousuf N, 1998, *Tomorrow's World: Britain's share in a sustainable future*, Earthscan/FoE, London; S Owens, 'Interpreting Sustainable Development', in Jacobs, 1997 (see note 1); *Opportunities for Change: consultation paper on a revised UK strategy for sustainable development, Department of the Environment*, Transport and the Regions, London, 1998.

3. On the idea of 'fair shares in environmental space' see Carley M and Spapens P, 1998, *Sharing the World: Sustainable living and global equity in the 21st century*, Earthscan, London; McLaren et al, 1998 (see note 2).

4. Burke T, 'The buck stops everywhere', *New Statesman*, 20 June 1997.

5. On new approaches to business accountability for environmental and social/ethical impacts, see Elkington J, 1997, *Cannibals without Forks: The triple bottom line of 21st century business*, Capstone, Oxford; *Environmental and Social Reporting*, Pensions and Investment Consultants (PIRC), London, 1998; Zadek S, Lingayah S and Murphy S, 1998, *Purchasing Power: Civil action for sustainable consumption*, New Economics Foundation, London.

6. *Local Agenda 21: The first five years*, Local Government Management Board, London, 1997; *It's a Small World*, Audit Commission, London, 1997; Selman P, 1998, 'A real local agenda for the 21st century?', *Town and Country Planning*, vol 67, no 1.

7. See *Rethinking the Good Life*, Demos, Demos Collection 14, London, 1998 forthcoming; Singer P, 1994, *How Are We to Live? Ethics in an age of self-interest*, Mandarin, London; Worpole K, 1997, 'A green space beyond self-interest', *New Statesman*, 30 May.

8. Solomon J, 1998, *To Drive or to Vote? Young adults' culture and priorities*, Chartered Institute of Transport, London.

9. See for example the report of the Real World Coalition of environmental and social campaign groups and other NGOs.

10. On eco-modernisation and cleaner production, see: Jackson T, 1996, *Material Concerns: Pollution, profit and quality of life*, Routledge/SEI, London; von Weizsäcker E, Lovins A and Lovins L, 1997, *Factor Four: Doubling wealth, halving resource use*, Earthscan, London; Gouldson A and Murphy J, 1997, 'Ecological Modernisation: restructuring industrial economies', in Jacobs, 1997 (see note 1); Christie I and Rolfe H, 1995, *Cleaner Production in Industry*, PSI, London.

11. On environmental taxation, see: Tindale S and Holtham G, 1996, *Green Tax Reform*, IPPR, London; O'Riordan T, ed, 1997, *Ecotaxation*, Earthscan, London. The Demos Working Cities programme, led by Robin Murray and Keith Collins, will produce a number of reports in late 1998 and early 1999 on the potential for job creation and new economic development at community level through recycling ventures.

12. Myers N, 1998, *Perverse Subsidies*, International Institute for Sustainable Development, Winnipeg; Chesshire J, 1997, 'Regulating the energy sector' in Greene O and Skea J, eds, *After Kyoto: Making climate policy work*, Special Briefing No. 1, ESRC Global Environmental Change Programme, University of Sussex.

13. See for example Macnaghten P et al, 1995, *Public Perceptions and Sustainability in Lancashire*, Lancashire County Council, Preston.

14. Huckle J and Sterling S, eds, 1996, *Education for Sustainability*, Earthscan, London; Carley M and Christie I, 1992, *Managing Sustainable Development*, Earthscan, London.

15. See *National Environmental Policy Plan 3*, Government of the Netherlands, den Haag, 1998. On Dutch approaches to eco-regulation, see Wallace D, 1995, *Environmental Policy and Industrial Innovation: Strategies in Europe, the US and Japan*, Earthscan/RIIA, London.

16. Held D, 1995, *Democracy and the Global Order*, Polity Press, Cambridge; Choucri N, ed, 1995, *Global Accord*, MIT Press, London; Archibugi D, Held D and Köhler M, eds, 1998, *Re-imagining Political Community*, Polity Press, Cambridge.

17. Levett R, 1998 'Rediscovering the public realm', *Town and Country Planning*, vol 67, no 1; Healey P, 1997, *Collaborative Planning: Shaping places in fragmented societies*, Macmillan, London; Teles S, 'Think local, act local', *New Statesman*, 22 August 1997.

9

THE FAMILY WAY: NAVIGATING A THIRD WAY IN FAMILY POLICY

Helen Wilkinson

The potential for a Third Way is strikingly evident in family policy: with the advent of the Labour Government a significant shift in thinking began to take place. At first sight, New Labour's approach to family policy has been to steal as many Conservative clothes as possible. In fact, New Labour in power has been far more pragmatic and keen to distance itself from 'top-down' moralising about family forms and values. The emphasis has been on seeking practical solutions to problems. But more important, New Labour appears to be searching for a new set of family values, which are distinct from the tired debates between conservatives and liberals that have dominated discussion of the changing family in Britain over the last few decades. In theory, this Third Way in thinking about families – 'the family way' – avoids retracing the faultline between liberals and traditionalists. In what follows, I explore this shift in thinking, and suggest how debates about family policy could evolve in the first decades of the twenty-first century.

TROUBLE AND STRIFE

Many families today experience huge strain. Relationships are breaking down at a rapid rate; more and more children are growing up in disrupted families; birth rates are in decline; and there is a serious tension for many between the demands placed on them to be good parents and spouses and to be high achievers in an increasingly competitive workplace. Our very notion of family itself appears to be threatened. The long-term trends suggest that we are not only living in a 'post divorce' society (in which divorce is commonplace), we are rapidly moving to a 'post marriage' one where marriage itself is increasingly redundant. (The first-time marriage rate is at its lowest possible level since 1889 and cohabitation is a cultural norm).[1]

There is a direct public policy interest here. Finance is a major factor. Weakened families cost the state money both directly and indirectly. In this context the state has a public interest in strengthening families, regardless of their structure. But political interest in families goes deeper. Families are the foundation of civil society, where we first learn moral values. Families generate social capital – the trust and relationship skills which enable individuals to cooperate. Family breakdown is a major factor in declining social capital and wider social dysfunction. The state has an interest and a role in preventing this.

But there is also a broader argument. The future growth of the economy, the vibrancy of our community life and culture, and the well being of tomorrow's retirees – all depend on how well families manage to raise the children who will become the citizens and workers of tomorrow. In short, the state has an interest in the capacity of our nation's children to thrive.

A TIRED DEBATE

In spite of this critical role, (or indeed perhaps because of it) debates about family life have a 'manic depressive' quality. On the one hand, conservatives lament the trends in family life. On the other, liberals celebrate the greater freedom that has accompanied these changes. Discussions about enhancing the well-being of our children and about strengthening families get lost in the fruitlessly polarised arguments between these positions.

Neither perspective fully comprehends the dynamics of change. Liberals downplay the costs of social change, while traditionalists misread lessons from history. In reality, the story is of decline and progress. Family change has brought greater freedom and autonomy but this process has not been without costs, and these have been borne most clearly by children.

There has been an unhealthy polarisation between liberals who affirm individualism and tend to take a relativist view of family values and structures, and between conservatives who talk a lot about values but neglect household economics. The result? A policy impasse. Yet we have been presented with a false choice. The problems being experienced by families today are rooted both in economic stress (whether of time or money) and in family disintegration. Any progressive family policy must address both these issues or it will fail.

We are just beginning to understand the full range of costs that society bears when families raise children less effectively than they can. The time is ripe for a progressive child-centred family policy which acknowledges the new realities and affirms enduring values. The challenge for government in the twenty-first century will be to find ways of stabilising families in an era of globalisation and enhancing their child rearing capacity, without imposing severe burdens on taxpayers and the state.

The American experience

America hit problems sooner than European countries did, and has innovated sooner. The running was first made by the Republican right with the then Vice-President Dan Quayle's infamous 'Murphy Brown' speech in 1992 when he criticised the fictional TV character, Murphy Brown, for bearing her children out of wedlock. To Quayle, this single parent symbolised a libertarian culture which was fast eroding traditional family values.

Quayle's speech was greeted with outrage from liberals, but within a few years there had been a shift in position. Barbara Dafoe Whitehead's article, 'Dan Quayle was right', published in the *Atlantic Monthly*,[2] reviewed the research literature and argued that there was a link between family structure and family outcome, regardless of poverty. Emerging data on the role of family structure in individuals' capacity to thrive precipitated a rethink within the Democratic party.

But the Democrats have drawn a new set of policy implications from recent research. They are unwilling to be held hostage to past ideologies or political correctness and recognise that the key to the development of sustainable and progressive family policy for the future would be the party's capacity to digest some home truths (such as the tendency for better performance of children in two-parent families) while at the same time seeking to avoid policies, as advocated by some Republicans, based on shaming those who do not conform to a traditional family model.

The Democrats have used family research to recast the whole family values debate. This meant understanding the constraints on working parents – the majority of whom are working and holding down unglamorous jobs and trying to make ends meet whilst caring for ageing parents and growing children. It meant recognising that families today are working on tight budgets of money and time and that they will welcome (and indeed vote for) a party which promises support through policies such as parental leave and subsidised child care.

The emphasis has been on fostering change in values and attitudes. The goal of social policies should be economic security and opportunity for American families and the reinfrcement of mainstream moral sentiments about family integrity, individual responsibility, and the mutual obligations of individuals and the national community. Healthy families are regarded as the foundation for a healthy society. According to the political theorist Theda Skocpol, 'Progressives need not adopt a morally relativist stance – we can champion moral understandings and practical measures that acknowledge the complexities that all Americans live on a daily basis.'[3] Progressives are being encouraged to acknowledge the tension that exists between ideals and second best necessities: this means working with families as they really are, whilst still striving for ideals such as more stable marriages and lower divorce rates.

NEW LABOUR, NEW FAMILY POLICY?

In his 1997 conference speech, Tony Blair stressed that success in strengthening family life would be a litmus test of his premiership, stating that every policy initiative would be measured by its capacity to strengthen family life. These bold claims underline the extent to which Tony Blair has been willing to move to a new position and break with the attitudes of previous generations of politicians who have been in denial about the changing cultures of family life. His own status also personifies a change in family life: the Blairs have a strong symbolic appeal as a modern dual-career couple juggling with the demands of work and a young family.

Like the Democrats, New Labour has been keen to take account of research on family life and to show that they are not hidebound by past ideology. Government pronouncements on marriage and the virtues of two-parent families have made it clear that these are ideals to be worked towards, but that families will be supported in all shapes and sizes. Walking a fine line between coercion and moral persuasion, the approach has the makings of a new consensus on family policy. However, the detailed policy implications of New Labour's family thinking have yet to be thrashed out, still less the indicators by which they will be judged.

Difficult unanswered questions stand out. If families are becoming more important than ever before, how can they be strengthened? We need a new way of thinking about families to inform policy decisions in the next century. What might this be?

THE PUBLIC HEALTH DIMENSION OF FAMILY POLICY

The 'traditional family' – and by this I mean the male breadwinner/female homemaker plus two children – is now a minority form and far too limiting as a model for family policy. But defining the 'best' type of family unit is extremely difficult. For policy makers, perhaps the simplest solution to the question of which model of family life to work with is to go back to first principles and to state that where there are children, there are families, whether they are intact or disrupted, and that the wider community has an interest in their thriving.

In general, most discussion of family issues assumes too rigid a division between different family forms. Too little attention has been paid to the links between 'traditional' and 'non-traditional' families and the transitions between them that people may make over a lifetime. We need to overcome such polarities. The aim should be to work with and strengthen disrupted families, whilst simultaneously working towards enhancing and promoting stable two-parent relationships in the context of marriage. Or, as John Gillis puts it in his book *A World of Their Own Making*, it means recognising the 'gap that exists between the families we live in and the symbolic families we live by'.[4] There should be less emphasis on coercion and moral exhortation and more on promoting the conditions for cultural change; less emphasis on what government can do and more on what it can help others achieve.

Families are generators of public health (and conversely of ill-health). It is inside families that we learn to trust, to form secure attachments, to be intimate with others whilst at the same time protecting each other's boundaries. Once we recognise that stable families are an essential element of stable communities, we can begin to develop social policy with the goals of strengthening and preserving families. Through this emphasis on the public health dimensions of family life, the benefits of sound families can be assessed, as can the level of dysfunction.

This public health approach to family life has a number of virtues. It allows us to sidestep the gender faultlines which have all too often stymied debates over family policy. At the same time, it gives us a general framework within which policies as disparate as parental leave and welfare-to-work can be connected, since in all cases family health (particularly child well-being) is a key aspect of the experiences we are measuring. Ultimately we will measure success in family policy on a range of holistic, long-term indicators, such as the following: lower divorce rates, longer adult couple relationships; an increase in the marriage rate, the strength of child/parent attachments; greater mental health; reduced illness; less alcohol and drug abuse; less absenteeism, and higher educational attainment.

FRONTIERS OF FAMILY POLICY

There are two large-scale and interwoven problems which need to be addressed if we are fully to understand the way in which families are changing as we move into the twenty-first century. The first is the need to strengthen intact families to help minimise the risk of break-ups and dysfunction. The second problem is family disintegration caused by divorce and relationship breakdown. This trend needs to be tackled directly because family breakdown carries with it a public health cost for all concerned. This is exacerbated by the culture of exclusion in the most deprived urban areas, where families are at high risk of fracturing or not cohering in the first place. Strengthening fragile families will be critical if we are to grapple with the causes of social exclusion and stand a chance of stopping the transmission of poverty and insecure attachment from one generation to the next.

1. Strengthening intact families

Tomorrow's politicians should try to strengthen intact families in various ways. The emphasis should be on ensuring that working families benefit from high quality subsidised child care, from varieties of paid parental leave, and from a 'family-friendly' tax and benefits system. Government will look to employers to play more of a role in facilitating changes in the culture of workplaces. Public–private partnerships will become commonplace as government seeks to place a share of financial responsibility for family life on taxpayers and employers in recognition of the fact that individual parents have paid too high a price in recent decades in foregoing income and advancement at work to take on the role of child-rearing.

The public health perspective requires that we make investments now in child care in order to reap benefits over the long term in reduced incidence of family breakdown, delinquency and exclusion, and increased levels of work satisfaction and performance, family cohesion and educational attainment. Welfare-to-work strategies need to be combined with schemes of paid parental leave, enabling parents to spend time with their family in the early years (critical for child health and family bonding) while at the same time giving unemployed individuals the opportunity to move into the labour market. In areas of social exclusion, where the numbers of people forming traditional intact families are in most serious decline, targeted welfare-to-work policies will be a vital means of giving individuals the economic stability to think about family formation.

Such economic measures should be combined with voluntary relationship and parenting programmes. The American experience suggests that the most innovative programmes have been rooted in the communities they serve, administered and designed by local community agencies which can foster the necessary trust and commitment with their clientele to make such schemes successful.

To date, welfare reform has been framed with adults' needs in mind. Tomorrow's welfare reform agenda will need to be 'child-friendly'. Just as working parents should benefit from genuine choices between high quality child care or parental leave, so too unemployed parents should benefit from welfare reform which recognises the value of family cohesion. The parental care credit advocated by Malcolm Wicks MP as an adjunct to government welfare-to-work strategies for single parents should be integrated into the next generation of New Deal options, driven by notions of equity and choice, and by public awareness of the importance of parental involvement in the early years of a child's life.

Attention will focus increasingly on enhancing fathers' role in family life, not just in providing for the family, but also in caring for children. Paid parental leave schemes will be one step in the right direction, but we should also anticipate innovations such as the establishment of a fatherhood task-force (modelled on task-forces and 'fatherhood commissions' in some American states) in imaginative efforts to raise public awareness about fathers' responsibilities as nurturers. Such a task-force's remit would be to review family policy across the board to assess how far specific measures and bureaucratic cultures help raise the profile of fatherhood and contribute to positive outcomes.

2. Strengthening the ties that bind in disrupted families

Tomorrow's politics of the family should aim to strengthen families disrupted by divorce or other breakdown, with children's well-being at the heart of policy. Recent reforms have been based on the view that whilst marriage may no longer be for life, parenthood is, and that so far as possible children should not suffer for their parents' mistakes. This emphasis on parental responsibility and managing the 'good break-up' is a pragmatic response to the new realities. It means starting with families as they are, rather than with how we wish them to be. Family policies should not be seen as a zero-sum game between two competing ways of living.

This approach should continue. Its success should be measured in terms of its impact on family health: its capacity to minimise conflict during and after relationship breakdown; the extent to which it facilitates father involvement; its impact on child well-being and so on. Informed by an awareness of the health impact on adults and children affected by family breakdown, policy-makers should focus on identifying effective ways of resolving unsatisfactory relationships as well as maintaining healthy attachments between parents and the child, regardless of the relationship between the adults.

Pressures to reform the system of child support will mount because of awareness in the policy making community of the costs incurred (financial and emotional) when fathers are not present in the lives of their children, perhaps especially of boys. Measures aimed at strengthening the ties that bind non-resident fathers to the lives of their children will rise to the top of the domestic policy agenda. Typically women have been the 'gatekeepers' to family life and because they have frequently had negative experiences with these men, they are reluctant to allow them back into their lives. However, American experience suggests that it is possible to forge a new consensus. Innovative 'team parenting' initiatives have achieved some degree of success in involving fathers and mothers as stakeholders in their children's future and could be tried out in Britain.

Effort should be focused on low-income non-resident fathers via welfare-to-work schemes which integrate personal and social skills training. Evidence to date from various innovative schemes in American states suggest that such programmes have wide appeal both for their employment and educational component, provided that participation is not forced on fathers. (Such an approach is not incompatible with tougher more rigorous enforcement of child support enforcement for the genuine 'deadbeat dads', the fathers who can pay but won't).

Complementing such experiments could be attempts to develop a single point of access for dealing with the public consequences of the break-up of a household – finance, access and visitation issues – regardless of the marital status of the couple concerned. A number of innovative US states are experimenting with such approaches.

If the American experience is anything to go by, the makers of tomorrow's family policy will bring fathers into the equation in unprecedented ways. The whole direction of family policy, which has historically marginalised fathers and focused on the mother/child dyad, should be reframed. The emphasis should be as much on shifting attitudes to family life and fatherhood within the bureaucracies and community at large, as on specific policies for supporting families.

LONG-TERM AGENDAS: TWENTY-FIRST CENTURY FAMILIES
Tomorrow's familiy policies will also need to grapple with three secular trends: the shift to the *post-divorce society* (in which divorce is commonplace); the shift to the *post-marriage society* (where the role and function of marriage is increasingly called into question) and the *growth in childfree families* (witnessed by the declining birth rate). In pursuing a public health strategy in family policy, we may need to seek ways to slow down, or even reverse, these movements.

These are grand goals demanding long-term strategy. But how are they to be achieved? What role should government play in promoting marriage, reducing resort to divorce and dealing with parenting issues?

1. Relationship building
Just as tomorrow's adults need the skills and competencies required to cope in an increasingly flexible and competitive economy, so too they need a more robust set of interpersonal and communication skills to cope with

more demanding and fluid personal relationships. The challenge will be to create opportunities to learn – rather than programmes relying in vain on coercion or moral exhortation. Classroom education, soap opera wisdom, counselling and advice services will all play a part.

Tomorrow's family should be a learning family and lifelong learning about relationships will be key. As we graduate from the classroom into adult life, we should be encouraged to seek advice and help where possible through local community agencies which provide advice and information about relationships and parenting.[5] These should be part-financed by government, but independent of it.

In policy terms the focus should be more on preventive strategies. We need to spend more now on the basis that we will save later. This means investing in relationship and parenting skills together, given that the single most important determinant of successful childrearing is lack of conflict between parents. We also need to concentrate our energies on making successful long-term relationships more likely, not on making divorce harder.

Critics might argue that governments should not involve themselves in affairs of the heart: that relationships are private and should remain so. Preventive strategies in family policy recognise that the fall-out from broken homes imposes wider social costs, and that it is worth trying to reduce these through more holistic policies. This is why we have a collective responsibility to enhance our capacities to sustain stable and intimate relationships, and why government has a role in trying to improve citizens' chances of success in long-term relationships, without interfering unacceptably in private life.

2. New Marriage
The second major goal should be to foster a marriage culture. Here policy-makers must feel that they are swimming against the tide. Marriage rates are in decline and the first-time marriage rate is at its lowest level ever. Yet, in the early decades of the next century, the promotion of marriage could rise up the agenda in policy circles, as the public health argument in favour of marriage becomes better understood and the research evidence more widely known.

Signs of a shift are already discernible. The government has shown that it is not afraid to talk about marriage, nor indeed to state their belief that the family headed by a married couple remains the most stable unit for rearing children that we have. But so far, New Labour's justification for supporting marriage has been framed in defensive, almost apologetic terms. The government is still relying on a 'deficit-based' approach to family issues. In a recent speech Lord Irvine, the Lord Chancellor, said that the government had a duty to give strong support for marriage and family life given the costs of divorce and family breakdown. Such justifications are hardly a ringing endorsement for the virtues of marriage. The language of the divorce culture still frames our debates.[6]

It is not hard to see why the government is defensive. Family policy is a highly charged and emotive area of debate, one in which the gulf between political rhetoric and personal practice can seem almost unbridgeable. Politicians always run the risk of sounding hypocritical or having their own family histories thrown back at them and this makes them cautious. But there are benefits from a more open and honest reflection on the issues which draws appropriately on personal experience. The Home Secretary Jack Straw has shown a capacity to lead in this manner. In speaking of the need to enhance relationship skills and competencies, he has drawn on his experience of divorce to reinforce his arguments. The challenge for tomorrow's politicians will be to combine openness about personal problems and family histories with political agendas, integrating the personal and political to great effect.

Although Jack Straw has begun to open discussion on the benefits of marriage, the wider public health argument needs to be more clearly stated. For successful and stable marriages do not just enhance the well-being of children, they benefit the adults concerned, generate good health and at their very best enhance the social and cultural capital of the individuals concerned. People in successful marriages are on balance healthier and happier than those who are single or unmarried. They also tend to be better off, and to have a denser network of connections to the community.[7]

In this sense, marriage helps build and sustain social capital. As an institution, it can generate trust, a sense of belonging and the strong and secure attachments required to nurture individuals who can thrive throughout life. It follows that policy-makers should be concerned to include gay couples within their remit and to offer them the same rights to legal marriage as heterosexual couples, on the basis that commitment and trust between individuals should be encouraged and fostered regardless of sexual orientation. (Of course, none of this negates the validity of the reverse argument, namely that divorce for couples in unhappy marriages can also be better for all individuals concerned).

But through what mechanisms can marriage actually be encouraged? Once again, there will be no quick fix. The challenge will be to promote a modern marriage culture, not by restoring the stigma of divorce, but by emphasising the virtues of marriage and equipping people culturally for a new style of marriage. This shift could be promoted through education in schools, through financing marriage preparation, relationship and parenting services at local level, and through encouraging pre-nuptial agreements for money and goods, as developed extensively in France and America.

This is an ambitious programme of cultural change and it will mean discussing the principles underpinning marriage in the twenty-first century. For whereas marriage in the twentieth century is still defined by the concept of romantic love, twenty-first century marriage should be defined by the concept of partnership, with the implicit assumption that marriages require the cultivation of 'emotional intelligence', work and commitment to sustain. The government should try to raise citizens' and practitioners' awareness of the elements that go into building successful marriages via the education system and a range of local services. Such information could be summarised in 'Smart Marriage' information kits available to couples when first making enquiries about getting married through their local registration service or other community agencies.

The run-up to marriage and the ceremony itself could become a focus for new practices.[8] In order to make the commitment essential to marriage something that is sustainable and achievable, the whole process must be thought through and rendered meaningful. In a largely secular society we may need new forms of ritual for marriage preparation to complement those provided by established religions, but which may be meaningful to relatively few couples. In addition, wider take-up of voluntary marriage preparation sessions will be important. In the twenty-first century, we will need innovations in ritual and public avowal of relationships that can strengthen the commitment of couples to marriage and the wider responsibilities that come with marriage and parenthood.

We could, for example, encourage those unattracted by religious frameworks for marriage to write their own vows, to personalise their own ceremony. The marriage ceremony could become the first of a series of affirming rituals – it could become commonplace for couples to reaffirm, renew and renegotiate their marriage vows on the basis that even the best relationships need to be worked at. 'Marriage mentors' – people from the community whose mission is to volunteer as a source of advice, support and a reference point for services – could be a beneficial innovation. Other advice services should be widely available options to couples in trouble (and subsidised for low income couples).

What role does or should government money play in helping to recreate a marriage culture? Why should an unmarried couple in their twenties pay a subsidy to a married couple of the same age, as with the married couple's tax allowance? The public health arguments for marriage are clear. But with the rise of cohabitation, it is important that the same kinds of services that are available to married couples are also open to co-habiting couples, since it is both constituencies that governments must reach if they are to foster a marriage culture.

In practice, the resources for strengthening and supporting marriage are already available to us in the form of the married couple's tax allowance: they need to be redirected in more productive ways. For example preventive initiatives such as marriage preparation classes deserve more support by comparison with reactive, palliative measures such as divorce mediation. As a new pragmatism takes hold in family policy attention will continue to shift to ways of redirecting the revenue generated from reducing this allowance, whose contribution to a marriage culture is marginal.

But we need to be clear about priorities. Children should be first in the queue for resources regardless of parents' marital status. In my Demos study on paid parental leave I showed how a generous scheme could be financed by as little as one tenth of the value of the married couple's tax allowance, a policy measure which would do much to enhance family health and strengthen relationships.[9] But this would still leave plenty of money left over to finance marriage-friendly initiatives such as those outlined above. The emphasis should be on investing money to promote a marriage culture wisely and where it is most needed, especially among those at risk of social exclusion.

3. The new parentalism

The third trend which policy makers should seek to reverse is the declining birth rate. The prospect of declining birth rates has raised the spectre not only of inter-generational imbalances but the prospect that there will be insufficient workers to finance the care needs of the elderly. (The UK birth rate has been declining since the 1960s and one-fifth of women born in the 1960s are predicted to remain childfree). Reversing this trend will require a major cultural shift, what I call a 'new parentalism', and it will need to be underpinned by economic subsidies.

Experience suggests that if childrearing is expensive it will be discouraged. If it is affordable it will be encouraged. Over the last few decades, the costs of family life have been shared unequally by individual parents (and by women). Taxpayers and governments must share the burden in recognition of the benefits created by good parenting. We should see a progressive pro-natalism take root, with other stakeholders in society (tax payers, the state and employers) bearing more costs to reduce those borne by parents.

What does this mean in practice? In policy terms, it means matching rhetoric about family values with genuine investments. Paid parental leave is one of the few policy tools with a proven track record in helping to reverse declining birth rates. Here we should look not to America, where leave is unpaid, but to Europe. Scandinavian countries have seen a dramatic return to family formation since the 1980s as a result of generous paid parental leave, and innovations in parental leave elsewhere indicate how families and ultimately the wider community can gain from integration of family-friendly policies into the world of work, and into welfare-to-work programmes for socially excluded parents.

This demands serious thinking about influencing workplace cultures and entrenched expectations about men's and women's relative engagement in paid work and family life. Involving fathers and raising the status of fatherhood will be critical. Government should also aim to bring about a healthier, more sustainable balance between work and family life. This will involve long-term debate and information campaigns to help effect a gradual culture change in our workplaces and build up a genuine commitment among employers to integrating work and family life. In this respect, the present 'family friendly' employment agenda is not radical enough: differentiating between workers with families and those without can lead to an unhealthy tension between the two, creating more obstacles to the much-needed shift in working styles and practices in the mainstream culture of work. The challenge will be to reorganise work in such a way that as many people as possible can find ways to integrate work and home lives better, and not feel pressured by workplace demands into making choices about when or whether to have children. But a progressive pro-natalist strategy should go further. In the end our policies for family-friendliness in employment will depend how far we can foster a more child-friendly culture overall, radically affecting the design of our public spaces and our community facilities as well as our workplaces.[10]

A key element in this programme will be to think through new ways of valuing the work of parents. This involves recognising that parents are the primary educators for their children. Community agencies could be funded to run imaginative public awareness campaigns focusing on the importance of the early years for children's healthy development. Although there are clear educational benefits from such early child development, it could be the public health benefits which will in the end prove most compelling.

TOUGH CHOICES
Tomorrow's policy-makers face a particularly modern dilemma. In a fast-changing 'knowledge economy', the socialisation of children and young people as thriving workers and citizens demands much greater reserves of

parental and institutional support than ever before. This comes at a time
when many long-term relationships are exposed to strain, when men and
women face intense demands at work and when their capacities to spend
time on parenting and other family activities are being squeezed. If ever
there was a time when families needed strong social support, this is it. This
is why, in spite of the greying of our society, we should anticipate an inter-
generational redistribution of resources in favour of children and their parents.

Ironically, it has been the parties of the centre left, not the centre right,
who have led the way in thinking about ways to stabilise family life, who
have been 'conservative' in recognising the need foster strong families for
the good of children and the community as a whole. That they have done
so without taking the moral high ground and whilst avoiding nostalgia for
the past is no mean feat. As the Conservative party tries to make itself relevant to a new generation of voters, it too will have to revise its assumptions.
Conservatives will have to confront head-on the tension that exists between
two key strands of centre-right thinking: its economic liberalism and its
socially conservative moral agenda. For the great irony is that despite the
previous Conservative government's rhetoric of traditional family values,
globalisation combined with free market policies did much to destabilise
family life and erode the traditional family values which Conservatives have
claimed to defend. The lesson for the future is a simple one. Tomorrow's
governments should focus on valuing families, strengthening and stabilising
them in all shapes and sizes, not moralising about them.

NOTES

1. Helen Wilkinson, 1997, *The Proposal: Giving marriage back to the people*, Demos, London.

2. Dafoe Whitehead B, 1993, 'Dan Quayle was right', *Atlantic Monthly*, April 1993.

3. Skocpol T, 1997, 'Part one: a renewed social contract – a partnership with America' in *The New Majority: Towards a popular, progressive politics*, Yale University Press, New Haven.

4. Gillis J, 1996, *A World of Their Own Making*, Basic Books, New York.

5. For proposals on new information and advice services about relationships and parenting, see Ed Straw, 1998, *Relative Values*, Demos, London.

6. Dafoe Whitehead B, 1996, *The Divorce Culture*, Vintage, New York.

7. Waite L, 1997, 'Why marriage matters', speech given at Strengthening Marriage Roundtable, Washington DC, 23 June 1997; see also Wilkinson, 1997 (note 1).

8. On innovations in marriage ceremonies, see Wilkinson, 1997 (note 1).

9. Helen Wilkinson et al, 1997, *Time Out: The costs and benefits of paid parental leave*, Demos, London, contains a comprehensive analysis of parental leave policies and costings for variations on paid leave schemes

10. On public space, children and families, see two papers in the Comedia/Demos series The Richness of Cities: Ken Worpole, 1998, *Nothing to Fear? Trust and respect in urban communities*, Comedia/Demos, London; Katherine Schonfield, 1998, *At Home with Strangers: Public space and the new urbanity*, Comedia/Demos, London.

10

TOMORROW'S EUROPE

Mark Leonard

HOW EUROPE FITS INTO TOMORROW'S POLITICS

Tomorrow's politics needs to reach parts that yesterday's never even dreamt of. The globalisation of the industrial economy, of our communications systems, of crime, and of environmental problems means that many risks and opportunities cannot be dealt with by nation-states on their own.

Globalisation tells us that national governments can no longer guarantee of the basic things we need to survive and thrive – our physical security, economic opportunity, and a sustainable environment. It means that European national governments are an awkward size: in some ways too big to be really effective at providing services and civic identity, but also too small to operate independently in an increasingly inter-connected world.

In order to cope with these challenges, we need to change the way we think about politics – our horizons must be much wider than our national boundaries. Just as we are looking for new institutions of cooperation at a national level to help us pool risks and deliver welfare, we also need to develop instruments of cooperation beyond the national level, between countries.

The traditional answer to these new threats would be to look for strength and safety by creating a bigger country – in much the same way as German and Italian principalities came together to form new countries in the nineteenth century. Big states can effectively protect economic and physical security, by having large markets and big armies. They are less likely to squabble amongst themselves (as small states are prone to do). It was this vision of providing peace by eliminating nation states in Europe that inspired Monnet and other federalists in the aftermath of the Second World War.

But big countries are not a panacea. Many national institutions – such as those concerned with welfare – are already operating at too large a level nationally and would not be ineffective on a European scale. The national governments of big countries also tend to be very distant from the majority of their people. Small countries are often more effective in their governance because their governments find it easier to respond, to communicate, to understand public opinion. Above all, small states do not expect to be able to control the world, and so are often better at adapting to it. This flexibility is a major source of strength in a rapidly changing world. Indeed some of the most adaptable and competitive countries of recent times have been little more than city states – for example, Luxembourg, Hong Kong, Singapore.[1]

Moreover, the values and attitudes of Europe's citizens have changed substantially over the past 50 years. People today are more likely to travel across Europe, speak a second or third European language and eat food from other European countries than ever before.[2] They see a an emerging common culture, a shared history and geographical space, and a converging set of values; as a result, increasingly many feel truly 'European'. In fact, two-thirds of people in the UK say that they feel 'European' as well as British.[3]

More importantly, they are aware of the limits of their national governments' powers, and want to see the European Union play a role in solving problems that are too big for their governments to handle alone – problems without frontiers. A large majority both in the UK and the rest of the EU want decisions on foreign policy, measures to protect the environment, the fight against drugs and policies on science and technology to be taken at a European rather than at a national level. But these people are also very attached to their own countries and do not see a conflict between these two positions. A recent poll suggests that 60 per cent of European citizens think that the EU should be responsible only for areas that cannot be settled at a national level.[4]

In short, people want an institution which allows them to enjoy some of the benefits of big countries without paying the penalty of losing the identity and functions of their own countries. The European Union represents this 'third way' between being a small state and being a region of a European state.

However, in spite of this increased openness to Europe, the EU itself is less popular than it has been for a generation. Fewer than half of European citizens support their country's membership of the EU. Only four out of ten people think their country has benefited from EU membership. And citizens' nascent European identity has not translated into support for the Union itself (ironically, the places where a sense of a 'European' identity appears to be strongest – Poland and the Czech republic – are not even in the EU).[5]

Faced with these challenges, the debate about European integration has been short of convincing accounts of the future of Europe as a political space. The biggest barrier to solutions to the EU's legitimacy has been that people thought about European integration in the wrong way, and looked for solutions in the wrong places.

UNDERSTANDING EUROPEAN INTEGRATION
Those involved in building and theorising the European Union constructed something which is totally new. Not only did their vision extend beyond the traditional idea of a sovereign state, they also went far beyond the idea of an international organisation such as GATT or the OECD. They created a system of governance that is neither a simple pooling of activities between a set of sovereign states, nor a scaled-up version of the nation-state.

The EU has acquired many of the elements of a classic political system. First, it has formal rules for collective decision-making, the 'government of the EU'. One of the basic principles of the EU is that European community law has precedence over national law, which means that all national law can only be enacted if it is not in conflict with EC law. By interpreting these rules and showing where they over-ride national laws, the European Court of Justice has managed to create a constitution. This means that, within Europe, the traditional idea of a sovereign state is dead.

Secondly, the EU is far from being simply a bureaucracy for managing the technical dimensions of European integration. It has a role in the big socio-economic questions that dominate most political systems. The EU is now involved in nearly all the policy areas of government, all except for housing, domestic crime and civil liberties (though many people wrongly assume it is even involved in these issues through the European Court of Human Rights, which is not part of the EU system).[6] It is responsible for half of all legislation at a national level, and 80 per cent of economic and social legislation.[7] The resources it distributes through the structural and cohesion funds are significant, making up to 5 per cent of the GDPs of smaller countries. But the EU has an even bigger impact through the things it rules out.[8] The distribution regimes of member states have been severely constrained by mutual recognition and harmonisation in the single market, the convergence criteria for monetary union and the emerging social policy agenda.

However, the EU is dramatically different from a traditional European state. It does not have extensive powers of coercion, a hierarchical bureaucracy or a large welfare budget. This is because the member states have not transferred their sovereignty to a higher level. Instead they have organised mechanisms for pooling and sharing sovereignty. In fact, the EU is more like a network or ecology of organisations than a state.[9] The EU differs from a state in three major ways.

First, there is no central figure or body like a president or a governing party able to set the agenda and drive it forward. This is because a network does not have a centre of power, but rather a series of nodes through which power is distributed. Some of the nodes are national governments, but others are European institutions and European interest groups. The nodes are not all of equal power, but these inequalities change depending on what is being discussed, and what alliances are formed. The key point is that, no matter how unequal the different nodes are, they are all interdependent. No single node, no matter how powerful, can ignore the others, even the smallest, in the decision-making process.

This leads to the second difference. With a political system organised along a network, there cannot be a classic division of powers between an executive, legislative and judiciary.[10] Instead of separating powers between three institutions, in the EU, all the institutions jointly share the roles of executive, legislative and judiciary. They alternate in different policy areas and at different stages in the decision-making process. For example, the Council acts as an executive on long-term issues, setting the agenda and delegating power to the Commission. The Commission acts as an executive in the short term, for example on trade and agricultural policy. Under some procedures – such as the advisory and management procedures – the Commission is more powerful. In others – such as regulatory and safeguard procedures – the Council is more powerful. The European Parliament and European Court of Justice also have a role in many of these procedures.

The third difference between the EU and a classic political system is that the EU doesn't have a politics. By that I do not mean that there are no politicians or political issues, but that there are no genuine political contests at European level. The heart of a democratic system is conflict: different groups of people putting forward strategic programmes for the future and battling it out to convince the general public. In most democratic systems, people are presented with a choice between competing manifestos. These are, sometimes, supplemented with referendums or other methods of consultation to ensure that the policies of the government reflect the priorities of the people it is intended to serve. If the politicians do not live up to their manifestos or break their promises, the voters can always 'throw the bums out'. At the level of the EU, citizens neither get to vote for the people nor for policies they want. Instead, divisions are artificially constructed into contests at national level about more versus less integration, or different conceptions of the national interest rather than different ideas of Europe. This is true for all of the EU's institutions.

The most powerful and visible institution is the European Commission. In fact, many people think that the EU is the European Commission. This makes them think of the EU as a bureaucratic machine, rather than a political body. The Commission was, in fact, designed to be above the political fray. It was, in many ways, about saving European publics and politicians from themselves. Commissioners are therefore asked to swear an oath of allegiance to European integration when they take up office, and promise to leave behind any other ties – to their countries, political parties etc. However, in spite of this pledge, all European countries are desperate to keep 'their' commissioner which shows that they are not entirely independent. As an institution it consults widely with European interest groups and is more open to sectoral pressure than public opinion or party politics.

Surprisingly, although the European Council is made up of national ministers, there is no real Euro-politics there either. All decisions are formally taken in their name, but in practice 90 per cent of decisions are taken by national civil servants in informal policy networks that include organised interests, such as the European farming lobby, and national experts. The more contentious decisions are taken by ministers, but the pattern tends to be very similar. The people making policy and distributing subsidies are departmental ministers who do not have to raise the money they hand out. As a result, 'departmentalitis' is rife. Ministers tend to act more as glorified lobbyists for national or sectoral interests than as politicians outlining a strategic programme. When there are major divisions on the council they tend to be between those who support and oppose closer integration, or between different conceptions of the national interest. The classic example of this was the negotiation over the single currency, where there was no discussion of the implications of the convergence criteria for jobs or other social issues. Even the General Affairs Council of European foreign ministers, which meets at least once a month and is meant to plan strategically, is anything but strategic.

One reason for this is that there are practically no defining conflicts about the future of Europe at a national level. No general election has been won or lost over competing visions of Europe. When it does appear on the agenda it is not discussed in a party political way. The parties do not argue so much about what Europe should be doing, as about whether we should have an EU at all, and if so how much. The failure to discuss the details of European policies is replicated in the British Parliament, where ministers are not held to account for their European activities. Despite the fact that as much as half of British legislation is made in Brussels, only 4 per cent of parliamentary questions in Britain were on Europe in the last parliamentary session. British MPs seem happy to leave scrutiny of European legislation to the

40 or so MPs who sit on the two European legislation select committees. They tend to see European affairs as the continuation of diplomacy by other means, rather than as a vital part of our political system.

Direct elections to the European Parliament were established to make up for this lack of accountability and of European politics at a national level. Although the European Parliament is organised on party lines and is developing increasingly cohesive party groupings, there are a number of factors that stop it from supplying the EU with a politics. First, there is the fact that elections to the European Parliament tend to be fought on national rather than European issues, which means that people do not get to express their preference for a strategic European programme. Second, the European Parliament is not the body where strategic decisions about Europe are taken. Third, MEPs represent on average half a million voters each, which makes them very distant from their citizens. Finally, the Parliament's own procedures have been designed to prevent proper political divisions. On many of the important procedures – such as budgetary matters – it needs to have a two-thirds majority to reach agreement, which means that important decisions are reached by consensus rather than party competition. In essence MEPs exist in a nether world – disconnected both from their citizens and from national governments and parties. This means that the European Parliament has less, not more legitimacy than national governments.

The Problems

Most of the EU's problems are a direct product of its uniqueness as a political entity. This is because our ability to construct new institutions has consistently run ahead of our ability to understand them, legitimate them or make them more efficient. Each of the differences from traditional nation state structures and processes has a number of negative consequences. They can be broken down into nine problems for the EU's legitimacy and efficiency:

1. The EU spends most of its time and resources doing the things that most citizens don't see as priorities. Only one in ten Europeans – and one in twenty people in Britain – sees ensuring an adequate income for farmers, or Economic and Monetary Union as priorities, but the EU spends half of its budget on the Common Agricultural Policy, and has more meetings on EMU than anything else. This is partly because the system is complex, but above all because there no real Euro-politics and no party competition between different programmes for the future.

2. The EU is not seen as successful at spreading the benefits of member-
    ship to the mass of people. Most people don't think in terms of the indi-
    rect benefits of the single market. They see the direct benefits going to
    'marginal' groups – farmers, heavy industry and residents of underde-
    veloped regions. And the indirect benefits that are most tangible are
    most likely to be felt by people with high skills, and high incomes. In
    short, middle England, Holland or Spain are reluctant to support EU
    membership. This again ultimately stems from the fact that the EU's poli-
    cies are not decided by party competition, so there is little incentive to
    deliver tangible benefits.

3. Opinion polls show that eight out of ten people claim to know 'little' or
    'nothing' about the EU. This is partly because the EU's structure is
    remarkably complex and opaque, and partly because there are never
    any widely publicised arguments about the EU in terms which relate to
    them and their priorities. This is because political parties do not see it as
    a normal political domain.

4. The Commission is too open to lobbying by sectoral groups. This means
    that decision-making is often driven by producers' interests and loses
    strategic focus. This results in some of the gross distortions of EU poli-
    cy, such as the fact that almost half the EU budget is still spent on agri-
    culture every year. This is a direct result of the Union's lack of politics.
    Because the Commission is not elected and has not proposed a coher-
    ent political programme, it seeks to overcome its illegitimacy by inviting
    as many interest groups as possible into the decision-making process.

5. As an unelected body, the Commission at times lacks the confidence to
    take on member state governments, and so is not always effective at
    policing European legislation. These inhibitions are a direct result of the
    Commission's lack of legitimacy.

6. The Commission occasionally proposes measures that appear designed
    to please national governments and interest groups but which are inap-
    propriate for European-level decisions. Recent decisions on zoos, drink-
    ing water, working time, and tobacco advertising seem neither to con-
    tribute to reinforcing the single market, nor to solving cross-border prob-
    lems. This is also arguably a direct result of the Commission's lack of
    confidence in its democratic legitimacy.

7. The way the EU is funded is unfair, and encourages ministers to act irre-
    sponsibly. It is inefficient because the Ministers who spend the money
    do not raise it, so they have very little incentive to save money. It is
    unfair because some countries pay disproportionately more than others.
    Today Germany's net contribution is 25 times that of France, although
    its GNP is not that much larger, and the Netherlands pays six times as
    much as France, though its population is less than a third of the size.
    The fact that the EU has such an opaque and inefficient funding mech-
    anism is because it does not have the legitimacy to raise the funds its
    needs in the open. This is also due to its lack of politics: if the policies
    being pursued had been debated transparently and argued for persua-
    sively, or were based more plainly on the public's priorities, it would be
    possible to ask citizens to pay for them.

8. Only a third of Europe's citizens think that they can rely on European
    institutions to solve problems. This is a result of high-profile failures
    such as the EU's inability to prevent the bloody fiasco of Yugoslavia's
    break-up. The fact that there are a myriad of competing interests oper-
    ating in Europe makes it very difficult to develop clear policies to deal
    with major crises. The fact that political parties are not aggregating poli-
    cies into strategic programmes makes it even more difficult to act deci-
    sively.

9. The EU is suffering a leadership deficit. The EU now has less sense of
    direction and mission than at any time in its history. Peace, prosperity
    and democracy – the clarion calls which motivated the foundation of
    what is now the Union – have each lost much of their resonance as
    many EU citizens have come to take them for granted. In their place,
    European leaders have nothing to offer beyond vague aspirations of
    building a European superpower. The reason it is so difficult to chart a
    clear way forward is partly because there is no single source of power,
    and partly because there is no forum for debating competing political
    visions of the future.

MISUNDERSTANDING EUROPEAN INTEGRATION
The main reason that the EU's problems of identity, legitimacy and leader-
ship have got worse rather than better is that people have misunderstood
European integration and have looked for solutions in the wrong places.
There have been three dominant approaches to European integration, each
with its own agenda and its own solutions to Europe's legitimacy problems.

They have all had a big impact on the development of the EU over the past 40 years, and all share some blame for the EU's current problems.

For many years some people were determined to think of the EU as being like any other international agency – like GATT or the OECD. They think that decisions should be taken by sovereign national states, and that each country should be able to exercise a veto over any decision. They therefore see the institutions in Brussels, especially the European Commission, as 'invasive' and their legislation 'imposed'. Their solution to legitimacy problems is simply to repatriate power from Brussels to democratically elected governments at a national level. But without a body proposing and policing agreements at a European level, and arrangements to adopt decisions which are not supported by all member states, it would have been impossible to build the single market – let alone devise effective policies on areas such as the environment. It is for this reason that inter-governmentalists have supported the existence of the Commission, but they continue to see the national arena as the only place to have political disagreements and legitimate European decisions. Inter-governmentalism has no room for mobilising European citizens or a European politics. It sees the EU as a problem of international relations, not democratic governance.

The other way of looking at European integration has the vision of creating a federal system – re-creating the nation state at a higher level. They divide into two camps.

First, those such as Monnet who favoured an incremental approach: federalism through the backdoor. They see integration occurring in many small-scale policy areas which spill over into other areas and in the process win elites over to the cause of integration. Integration, for them, is an inexorable process that can be accelerated by building new institutions. The way to deal with legitimacy problems is to involve as many elites in different areas and countries as possible in the decision-making process, and encourage private lobbies to develop European levels of organisation. This was always a top-down process that was never interested in mobilising public support, or developing a politics.

The other approach is federalism by the front door. They see legitimacy at a European level in exactly the same way as they conceive it for the nation state. The way to achieve it is to develop a single source of power, divide it between a legislative, executive and judiciary and legitimate it through elections to a Parliament. Over the years, Federalism has succeeded in securing some political institutions – such as the European Parliament (more recently calls for citizenship, and the extension of EP powers). This approach does deal with some of the EU's blind spots. Unfortunately, it does so at a price.

Adopting a genuinely federal political system would destroy many of the things that make Europe special. It would take away its flexibility and diversity. It would create a politics, but at a further remove from the public. Above all, it would run counter to the preferences of most EU citizens. Any solution that is not based on the values and priorities of European citizens, as well as their sense of themselves, would not only be wrong, but also ineffective. The European Parliament's lack of success bears testimony to this.

THE SOLUTIONS

It would clearly be unwise to destroy the things we have gained through the creation of the EU by building heavy-handed institutions that centralise power. But, at the same time, the EU cannot afford to remain so far out of kilter with its people's priorities. Its lack of legitimacy could threaten its long-term future, and is already having a corrosive effect on its efficiency. In order to tackle the EU's deeper problems, we need fresh thinking about the politics of integration.

Any solutions must recognise that the EU needs to continue to be a network, an innovative ecology of collaborating organisations rather than a single source of power. So the challenge is to create a glue that is capable of binding together different parts of the European political ecosystem, to link them to their citizens and give them a sense of direction – and all that without destroying its subtlety. This boils down to a double challenge:

- Firstly, the EU needs to discover mechanisms to make the EU closer to the people it serves, and to ensure it does the things they want.
- Secondly, it needs to become more effective at doing them, and to appear to be more effective.

One institution that can go a long way to meet these aims is the political party. Though it has become fashionable to downgrade the role of political parties, there is as yet no other institution which exists solely to provide a link between the public and public policy. Although they have many problems, over the years they have proved themselves to be more effective at providing leadership, defining strategic goals, articulating the interests of different social groups, devising policy and mobilising citizens than any alternatives. Moreover, all the main families of political parties – social democrats, Christian democrats, liberals, greens and the far right – are represented in all political countries, and in all EU institutions. Across Europe, parties have become far more similar both in the way they organise and in their philosophies over the last few years. And since 1990, European Party leaders have held caucuses before major EU summits. The unique challenge faced by the EU has been to create a politics without a polity. It should be possible for parties to fill the gap – using their infrastructures to agree on strategic programmes, without building heavy-handed federal institutions to deliver them.

In order to do this, we need to agree on what the responsibilities of the EU should be, so that people can understand its role in their lives clearly. This will go some way to calming people's fears of invasion and homogeneity. Once we have agreed what Europe is for, we need to make changes to the way the EU organises itself. I propose eight radical steps which could be used to create constructive political conflicts at a European level and ensure that tomorrow's Europe is a people's Europe.

1. European Charter

A short charter on the EU could explain what the EU is for and contain a code of guidelines on what sorts of issues it should get involved in. This should explain that the EU is not about creating a super-state, but about strengthening its member states by allowing them some of the advantages that large states enjoy, including, a large unified market (with the powers to regulate competition); structures to give EU members influence abroad, both through soft foreign policy influence and military capability; Structures to tackle cross-border problems such as the environment, drugs and crime policy; and a framework for cooperation in other areas. It should also make it clear that the EU should be decentralised. It should keep spending at a national level, and recognise that in many areas it is worth preserving cultural and policy diversity for diversity's sake. Finally it should talk about the values the EU should embody: openness, accountability, fairness, competition, democracy, solidarity.

2. European Forum

We should establish a European Forum of MPs drawn from national parliaments as a means of plugging national parliaments into European decision-making and policing this code.

3. Direct elections and a reduced role for Commission

One powerful way to make sure that there are genuine debates about the future of Europe at a national level is to have an election about the future of Europe. Rather than pushing towards re-creating the parliamentary model on a European scale, one could directly elect the Commission on the basis of party slates. As the Commission is the only body that has the right to propose legislation, elections for this post would politicise the agenda and could ensure that people got to vote for a strategic programme. The candidates and slate would have to be nominated by at least one party in every EU country. It has been suggested that one could politicise the Commission by allowing the European Parliament to elect the Commission President, but this indirect route would be unlikely to have the resonance that direct elections would have, for all the reasons outlined above. If the President were directly elected, he or she would have far more legitimacy and authority. This would mean that Europe could become more efficient, but it would be an additional reason for defining the role of the Commission more carefully and restricting it to legitimate tasks.

4. Organise the Council along more partisan lines
The fourth step would be to organise the Council along party lines. This would mean organising caucuses of departmental ministers before meetings to agree a party strategy on the big issues of the day (this has been the practice for party leaders since 1990). It would also mean sitting according to party affiliation rather than alphabetical order in council meetings. This would require changes within the party infrastructures, but would not need any change to EU institutions.

5. Make the Council less segmented
By grouping issues rather than having each Council focusing on a single issue like agriculture, the Council could be made more strategic, more able to integrate different issues of policy, and less open to manipulation by sectoral interests such as the farming lobby.

6. National Ministers for European Affairs based in Brussels
We should consider establishing national ministers for European affairs in Brussels, and giving them a permanent secretariat there would be a recognition that Europe is a political sphere. It would engage national parliamentarians in European integration, and would provide a political slant to discussions previously left to officials. A regular meeting of this body could replace the General Affairs Council and provide real strategic planning for European integration.

7. Referenda on European issues
One positive way to make European citizens think of the EU as a body for solving problems would be to allow them to propose referenda on specific policies – either to propose or to block policies. If these were held simulta-

neously in all member states when a certain number of signatures in a certain percentage of member states were collected, they would move the debate on from a simple opposition between supporters and opponents of deeper and closer integration.

8. Making the EU's financial arrangements fair, open and more independent

The EU should take urgent action to end the gross unfairness of the current pattern of contributions to EU budgets. Unfair contributions are creating waves of Euro-scepticism in countries such as Germany. It should establish a new system that decides net contributions according to per capita GNP. We should also investigate the idea of allowing the EU to set hypothecated European taxes. If the EU had the power to finance itself, ministers and commissioners might act more responsibly, and it would also be able to become more effective and independent of member states.

CONCLUSION

We are only a few years away from the fiftieth anniversary of the Treaty of Rome. By almost any criteria this ranks as one of the most successful treaties ever signed. It has delivered steadily rising prosperity, and a civic underpinning for peace in a continent used to war. Europe's leaders succeeded in doing this by boldly inventing new institutions and taking on tasks that were considered impossible. But, with its initial goals largely accomplished, and new problems left unresolved, the EU is at risk of drift and lacks a coherent strategic vision beyond that of economic union. In its next phase Europe needs to re-invent itself again matching its ingenuity at devising new institutions with a bold programme to put them back in touch with the people they are designed to serve.

To do this, it needs to break free from established ways of thinking about Europe as an embryonic state or an international organisation. This article suggests a package of measures which could make the EU both closer to its citizens and more effective. They represent a new way of thinking about the politics of integration, and if implemented, they could create something even more innovative than the current EU: a politics without a polity.

Mark Leonard's book, *Europe's Political Deficit*, is published by Macmillan in summer 1999.

NOTES

1. Peter Mandelson MP made this point eloquently in a speech to a seminar that was organised by the British Embassy in Bonn.

2. Leonard M, 1998, *Rediscovering Europe*, Demos, London.

3. See note 2.

4. Leonard M, 1997, *Politics without Frontiers*, Demos, London.

5. See note 2.

6. See note 4.

7. See note 4.

8. Hix S, 1998, 'The study of the European Union: The 'new governance' agenda and its rival', *European Public Policy*, March 1998.

9. Castells M, 1998, *The End of Millennium*, Blackwell, Oxford.

10. See note 8.

11

PARIS, BONN, ROME:
A CONTINENTAL WAY?

Frédéric Michel and Laurent Bouvet

*'Yes, there is a Third Way. The United States under the Clinton admin-
istration is trying to do this. For a lot of people in the first half of the
century, government was the answer. For that period it was the correct
answer. Then the right came along and said the answer was to get rid
of government. The essence of the Third Way is to say that the role of
government is to organise and secure provision rather than fund it
all. For example, in pension reform, people will have to provide more
of their own financial independence, but government has a role in
organising that system'*

Tony Blair, *Time*, 27 October 1997

Since Labour's May 1997 victory, Tony Blair seems to be setting the tone of
European politics. Alongside him, his main European social-democrat col-
leagues Lionel Jospin, Romano Prodi and Gerhard Schröder appear old-fash-
ioned. But with centre-left parties in the ascendant in Europe, Blair's high
visibility has put him in a powerful position – and the British prime minister has not shrunk from claiming a leadership role in Europe's political
future. Whether they like it or not, other centre-left leaders in Europe must
compare themselves and be compared with Blair.

When that comparison is made, it focuses attention upon an overarching
question: is Blair's proposed Third Way, an acknowledged import from
Clinton and the New Democrats, one towards which the Continental centre-
left is willing to move? Or is it a diversion, the effect of which will be to
allow Britain to keep its distance from the mainstream of European politics,
as it did under Margaret Thatcher? In other words, is the Third Way a project for Europe, or for Britain and the United States?

The critical proving ground for this argument is in France and Germany,
both of which could have governments of the left by the time this essay is
published, and around whom the European Union has been constructed.

Will the real Lionel Jospin stand up?

Viewed from Paris, the prospects for the Third Way do not appear to be so good. The context of Jospin's election victory last year could not have been more different from Blair's. The British prime minister has a massive parliamentary majority in a system which confers huge power on his office. Jospin heads a diverse coalition, in a presidential system, and the current President is a member of the country's conservative opposition party. Jospin's Majorité Plurielle contains five parties, the Socialists, the Communists, the Greens, the Mouvement des Citoyens (a small, Eurosceptical republican-nationalist party with a strong critique of globalisation) and the Socialist Radical-Party (PRS), which resembles the British Liberal Democrat party.

The only strong link between all these parties is a collective search for positive image after periods in the political wilderness; the result is not always coherent in policy-making. For example, the closure of the Superphenix nuclear plant and the implementation of the 'clean air' law were clear concessions to the Greens, but an increased road-building programme was designed to appeal to the Communists and was denounced by Les Verts. At the Amsterdam summit, Jospin balanced his coalition's competing interests to keep France loyal to the project of the single currency and the same balancing act can be seen in sensitive areas like privatisation and policy towards immigrants. The aim is to hold the coalition together, putting further pressure on the right.

But to understand the strategic direction of the French left, it is necessary to look at what was going on before Jospin's election victory in 1997 and how this is likely to be affected by the compromises of the 'Majorité plurielle' in government. At his party's recent congress, Jospin described his approach as 'volontarisme realiste' (effective translation: pragmatism), contrasting it with the inflexible 'realisme de gauche'. He speaks of 'a new political synthesis' on the left, imagining the Socialist Party as the central pillar of this new hybrid, committed to 'social transformation, a return to a republican tradition, a deepening of our democracy and more equality between men and women'. In spite of the precariousness of his coalition, Jospin has, in fact, made headway with all these agendas, some of which connect with the agenda of Blairism, such as electoral reform and cleaning up politics; others, such as the 35-hour working week and a proposed 'republican pact with the citizens' are far beyond the British horizon.

Perhaps the most revealing area of policy, in terms of volontarisme realiste has been Jospin's handling of the complex brew of labour disputes and privatisation, which came to a head in June in the Air France dispute when, after a ten-day strike costing the airline $160 million, the main pilots' union capitulated and agreed to cut costs by holding down wages. The pilots had banked upon backing from the Socialist Prime Minister, but Jospin came out firmly in favour of the Air France plan, while refusing to involve himself in detail. The airline is now expected to be able to cut its wages bill by 15 per cent in the next seven years, to help finance a $6.7 billion modernisation plan. The Communist Transport Minister, Jean-Claude Gayssot has vowed that he will never be the 'Minister of Privatisation', but the pressures of the market and of EU resistance to state subsidy are likely to push Air France into the private sector in the long run. Jospin's support for the partial privatisation of France Telecom indicates a pragmatism which is more Blairite than it is Old Labour, but it is still some distance from Blair's statements during the British general election campaign that wherever possible, private sector solutions would be favoured over the public sector.

Jospin's presumed goal is to follow a successful spell as prime minister with a bid for the Presidency in 2002. He is unlikely to achieve that by lurching towards an Atlanticist model of liberalism – hence his care to distinguish himself from Blair and to emphasise the traditional virtues of European social democracy – a strongly regulated economy, strong welfare state, well-funded public services and sustained state involvement in the business sector. At the root of the difference between Jospin and Blair is a difference of philosophical tradition. The British political tradition, which arises from Adam Smith, John Locke and John Stuart Mill, predisposes it towards a greater flexibility towards the claims of markets and individualism than the continental idea of a negotiated social contract, with its roots in Jean Jacques Rousseau and Emmanuel Kant. Will Hutton, who may be more comfortable with Jospin than with Blair, has observed that 'the case for the social-democratic model is that it promoted social solidarity, is a rational response to life hazards and is a vital support system for every citizen necessarily confronted by the instability and inequity of capitalism'. Or as Jospin himself has put it, he wants a market economy ('une economie de marche)' but not a 'market society (societé de marche)'.

It is noticeable that key figures on the French left, such as Pierre Mauroy (president of the Socialist International) and Michel Rocard (for long considered one of the most progressive French politicians) have warned against Blair's 'Third Way'.

Those who have taken a close interest in the Blair programme, such as the independent think tank the Fondation Saint-Simon, tend to be portrayed as liberal, rather than of the left and it is a fact that some of Blair's most effusive admirers in France come from the right, such as Alain Madelin's Democratie Liberale Party. No one will easily forget that during Blair's famous address to the Assemble National, he was cheered by the Conservatives, not the Socialists.

HERR SCHRÖDER AND THE 'NEW MIDDLE'

In Germany, the SPD leader Schröder avoids the term, the Third Way, but he is keen to recognise the emergence of a like-minded international fraternity of the centre-left. His preferred slogan is the New Middle, distancing himself from the mistakes of his predecessors. Oskar Lafontaine, the SPD challenger to Kohl in 1990, who lost the confidence of the key West German electorate when he promised to slow down the privatisation of former East German industries to protect the workers. Schröder preaches the need for the private sector to become more competitive and flexible by cutting labour costs. In 1994, in an equally unsuccessful run against Kohl, SPD candidate Rudolf Sharping proposed higher taxes on middle and upper-middle income families. Schröder proposes cutting the highest income tax rate from 45 to 35 per cent.On pensions, he goes even further than Kohl and talks eventually about supplementing the creaking state system with private retirement funds and profit-sharing schemes along US lines.

The political strategy of this New Middle is obvious, seeking to appeal to younger and more affluent voters, including the self-employed. As with New Labour and the New Democrats, the stress is on 'modernity' and 'technological innovation'. Schröder has also explicitly picked up the Clinton-Blair welfare-to-work approach and the commitment to restrain public spending.

But there are also some crucial distinctions between Blair and Schröder, not least that the German economy is a powerhouse (albeit one with high unemployment) which has not been through Anglo-American style deregulation. If Schröder is to become chancellor, he must build from the legacy of the conservative Helmut Kohl, not the radical neoliberal Margaret Thatcher. Conversely, it is also true that the SPD made its historic accommodation with a mixed economy in 1959 at Bad Gödesberg, whereas the Labour Party hung on to its objective of nationalising the commanding heights of the economy until Blair tore it apart in 1995.

If elected, it is entirely possible that Schröder could embrace a recognisably Third Way agenda, pursuing left-of-centre values but opposed to big government and comfortable with the workings of the market. Given the pragmatism of other left-ish governments in Europe, from Sweden and Holland in the north to Italy and Portugal in the south, a German tilt towards the Third Way could be decisive.

Like Jospin, however, Schröder knows that he cannot realistically hope to govern without a coalition partner, if he is given the opportunity to govern at all. Alliance with the former Communists of the east is unthinkable to him, but he may not be able to avoid coalition with the Greens, unless conditions were to make possible an SPD-led Grand Coalition with the Conservatives, which may be Schröder's true preference, though not that of his party. Whatever the outcome of the election, Schöder is unlikely to be as free as Blair to ignore the left wing of his own party.

Another important difference between Blair and Schröder relies in the intellectual dimension of their political ambition. The British Labour Party leader understood from the beginning the necessity of a theoretical reconstruction of his own party's social-democratic doctrine, as a way of steering it towards a more market-oriented, liberal position. It is striking that a more or less informal network of think-tanks emerged to support this programmatic renovation – something which has given the United Kingdom a leading position in the European-American political debate. There is no equivalent in Germany to the activities of think tanks like Demos, the Institute for Public Policy Research and the Centre for European Reform and still less for the way that a leading university, the London School of Economics, has positioned itself as an intellectual reservoir for the project of the Third Way.

Schröder does not have the same ambition. Recent 'brainstorming' on the renovation of social-democracy in Germany has taken place inside official and less flexible academic structures, such as the Friedrich Ebert Foundation or the Max-Planck Institute. And as Robert Leich has pointed out:

> 'Schröder welcomes comparison with Blair and thinks that liberalisation, even privatisation, is modernisation. He is popular among business leaders and talks about Anglo-Saxonisation of the German model (although this did not prevent him from nationalising a steel company in his own state to prevent job losses). Lafontaine, on the other hand, tends towards a more French, statist understanding of social democracy.'

In short, it is not clear that Schröder has negotiated permission inside his own party to pursue a Third Way strategy: the SPD and New Labour may well find themselves some distance apart.

BLAIRITE FRUITS OF THE OLIVE TREE

The influence of Blair's style on Romano Prodi's political behaviour is obvious. For example, Prodi is trying to set up in his headquarters at the Palacio Chigi a team of advisers modelled on the Downing Street Policy Unit.

But Prodi too must play coalition politics, heading Italy's first government of the left since the Second World War. The leader of Rifondazione, Fausto Bertinotti, has made his support for Prodi's Olive Tree alliance available only on a highly conditional basis, opposing the 1998 budget, for example, because it was making the tough budgetary cuts necessary for membership of the European single currency. Eventually, Rifondazione fell into line, in return for Prodi's promise to legislate for a 35 hour-work week starting in the year 2001 – a move bitterly opposed by business and questioned by some Italian unions. Senator Roberto Napoli of the minority Christian Democratic Center has spoken of the two lefts inside the coalition, one modern and the other still deeply connected to its Marxist roots. Tensions between Prodi and Bertinotti are severe, resulting in blockage of the prime minister's proposed reform of Italy's bloated pensions system.

Inside the PDS itself, the main party of the coalition, there are differences of view about the Clinton-Blair Third Way. Walter Veltroni, Minister for Culture and co-director of the Olive Tree, has made no secret of his admiration for the American Democratic Party. Meanwhile Massimo D'Alema, general secretary of the PDS, is jockeying to become the next Prime Minister, trying to gather around himself a new alliance of the left, on more classic social democratic lines.

D'Alema's objective is certainly intellectually ambitious: to create the theoretical basis for Italian social-democracy in the next century. The creation of a new reflexive organisation, under the name of Italianeuropei, headed by the former Prime Minister Giuliano Amato, which would include the Gramsci Institute (the traditional home of the Italian left for research and contact between the party and the intellectuals) is the most obvious sign. This new Foundation could very quickly become a think tank devoted to the political candidature of D'Alema as the successor to Prodi.

A NEW SOCIAL CONTRACT

One of the defining characteristics of European social democracy has been the way it has institutionalised political negotiation about the welfare state and wages. Given the constraints upon all members of the European monetary system, it seems likely that countries with strong social partner institutions – employers and unions – will use that route to seek consensus about reform, rather than attempting to beat opponents into submission in the manner of Margaret Thatcher. From a European standpoint, it is not yet possible to judge where Blair stands in this argument: on the one hand, he has proposed a minimum wage and increased rights of representation for unions and speaks of 'thinking the unthinkable' on welfare; on the other, he has shown no interest in reviving the apparatus of tripartite discussion of economic and social issues. On wages (where inflation is again a cause for concern), British ministers have resorted to the only tool available: making speeches and warning that the Bank of England may be driven to raise interest rates still higher.

Elsewhere in Europe, there have been some striking successes of the negotiated route to reform. The Dutch and Irish economies have enjoyed low inflation and greater than average growth as a result of social pacts and there are considerable hopes for the more recent Italian and Spanish pacts. In Italy, apart from contributing to the fulfilment of EMU entry conditions by subduing wage inflation, the social pact has covered measures to compensate those laid off in restructuring, rights for temporary workers, and assistance for the unemployed to enter the labour market. But it has also become the critical forum for bargaining over broader aspects of social regulation. The most significant steps in this regard were the agreements signed between the unions and the government on pension reform this year and last.

Schröder's strategy lies very much within this tradition; he has proposed an 'alliance for jobs and training', bringing together employers, trade unions and the government to produce measures to boost job creation and apprenticeships and reform the tax system. The acknowledged task in all these social democratic countries is to negotiate between the social partners in a context of increased global competitiveness.

It is important to note, however, that France is to some extent an exception to this tradition, because its trade unions are incapable of organising a significant portion of the French work force behind any bargain with government, with the result that the state invariably finds itself obliged to impose reform, or to back away for fear that the necessary consensus for change has not been achieved – very much the pattern of recent years. From this point of view, Jospin and Blair have more in common than Schröder and Jospin – a point which could have some significance in the period ahead. Perhaps this explains why some European leaders attempt to join both sides of the argument. For example, the Greek Prime Minister, Kostas Simitis, has spoken of the importance of building a bridge, in a 'new organisation', between the New European left and the American Democrats, as suggested by Blair, Clinton and Prodi. At the same time, he strongly supports the Socialist International and identifies with the Jospin project of 'social justice, democracy, and the state perceived as a headquarters which does not always and systematically intervene but regulates economic life.'

The likeliest outcome of this debate is that France and Germany, for different reasons, will settle for a modernisation of social democracy and will see the future of the European Union in those terms – a point of no small significance as the agenda post monetary union turns to fiscal harmonisation and, inevitably, greater concurrence of patterns of public spending. The question for Europe is whether a Germany and France pursuing modernisation of social democracy will meet a Third Way British government because they are, essentially, travelling in the same direction, but on board different vehicles. If this turns out not to be the case, a liberal Blairite Labour Party could find itself isolated in its own Third Way, with there is the danger that Blair comes to seem as alone in Europe as Margaret Thatcher.

It is in no one's interests, however, that this should be the case. What Blair's Third Way offers continental social democracy is a more realistic and urgent engagement with modified market liberalism – it represents an accommodation with real global forces, which will bear down upon Europe whatever happens to the Third Way and social democracy. American capitalism seems destined increasingly to dictate the terms of global trade. On the other hand, the attractions for Britain of pursuing a destiny as 'the Hong Kong of Europe', as some Thatcherites used to dream, looks even less attractive today than it did ten years ago. The point, surely, is that in plotting his Third Way, Blair needs to pay more attention to his social democratic neighbours to the east, just as they will be well advised to take him and his ideas seriously. A meeting of the Third Way and renewed social democracy looks like Europe's best story in the years to come.

For that to happen requires a political debate of a much more vigorous and open kind within Europe's centre-left – something which Blair deserves credit for sparking, even if he has sometimes been criticised for lack of tact. John Lloyd has written that the choice is between a 'crossing of traditional liberalism and social democracy' and a 'modernised, pragmatic but still recognisable centre-left.' It may not turn out to be such a choice after all.

BIBLIOGRAPHY

Adonis A and Pollard S, 1998, *A Class Act: The myth of Britain's classless society*, Penguin, London.

Blanchard O and Fitoussi J-P, 1998, *La Croissance pour Vaincre le Chomage: Elements d'une nouvelle politique*, Notes de la Fondation Saint-Simon, Paris.

Blitz J, 'Italy's sluggish growth', *Financial Times*, 22 August 1998.

Borioni P, 1998, *Socialismo Postmoderno: La societa aperta e il nuovo partito della sinistra*, Armando Editore, Roma.

Christie I, 1998, 'Sustaining Europe: A continent in search of a mission' in *EuroVisions: a new dimensions of European Integration*, Demos Collection Issue 13, Demos, London.

Crouch C and Streeck W, eds, 1997, *Political Economy of Modern Capitalism: Mapping convergence and diversity*, Sage, London.

D'Alema M, 1997, *La Sinistra nell'Italia che Cambia*, Fetrinelli, Elementi, Milan.

Ferrera M, 1998, *Le Trappole del Welfare State*, Il Mulino ˚ Contemporeana, Bologna.

Giddens A, 1998, 'After the left's paralysis', *New Statesman*, 1 May 1998.

Grant C, 1998, *Can Britain Lead in Europe?*, Center for European Reform.

Gray J, 1996, *After Social Democracy*, Demos, London.

Gray J, 1998, 'A strained rebirth of liberal Britain', *New Statesman*, 21 August 1998.

HuttonW, 1998, 'Until Blair decides whether he's a liberal conservative or a social democratic reformer....', *Observer*, 2 August.

'Le new Royaume Uni', *La Revue de la CFDT*, December 1997, No.5s.

Lazar M, 1998, 'La Gauche en Italie: le mariage du nouveau et de l'ancien'. *Le Debat.*, May-August, No 100.

Leadbeater C, 1997, *Civic Spirit: The big idea for a new political era*, Demos, London.

Leich R, 1998, 'What ever happened to the German-left?', *Prospect*, August/September 1998.

'Giovanni e Prodi', *Liberale*, 23 April 1998, pp 45-46.

Lloyd J, 1997, 'Everyone's talking about jobs', *New Statesman*, 27 June.

Lloyd J and Bilefsky D, 1998, 'Transatlantic wonks at work', *New Statesman*, 27 June.

Norman P and Atkins R, 1998, 'Teuton Titan and Teuflon', *Financial Times*, 21 August 1998.

Olivennes D, 1998, *Le Modele Francais: Un compromis Malthusien*, Notes de la Fondation Saint-Simon, Paris.

Rhodes M, 1998, *Globalisation, Labour Markets and Welfare State: A future of competitive corporatism?*, RSC, EUI, No.97/36.

Rosanvallon P, 1995, *La Nouvelle Question Sociale. Repenser l'Etat Providence*. Seuil, Paris.

Rosanvallon P and Fitoussi J-P, 1996, *Le Nouvel Age des Inegalites*, Seuil-Essais, Paris.

Smith P, 1998, 'Third Wave not drowning', *Chartist*, July-August.

Weber H, 1998, *Que reste-t-il de Mai '68? Essai sur les interpretations des evenements*, Seuil-Points, Paris.